Practical Emotional Intelligence

&

The Enneagram Of Personality

-2 In 1-

Why EQ And Personality Types Will
Help You To Grow And Develop In Ways
You May Not Have Ever Considered

By

Arthur Canfield

Table of Contents

Practical Emotional Intelligence

The Enneagram Of Personality

Practical Emotional Intelligence

Why Improving Your EQ Will Take You Further In Life And How To Do It

By

Arthur Canfield

Introduction

Ever since the concept first gained popularity, and as we all continue to understand it through the years, Emotional Intelligence has been growing away from being a mere "idea" to becoming a concrete facet of human behavior. Like any muscle in the body, emotional intelligence has become increasingly important to exercise and develop in our hopes of becoming better individuals. Yet, for many, the question still looms large: What is emotional intelligence?

In this book, you will not only begin to answer that important question by understanding the roles that our emotions, thoughts, and habits play into the development of emotional intelligence (EI). Learn all the important elements of this human ability and there you can glean the answer to the much bigger question of how to improve your emotional intelligence.

I'm sure that not a few will agree that this significant ability to recognize, understand, and eventually manage one's emotions has become a crucial part of daily living. The web of human emotions can be quite complex and tricky to navigate in the aim of establishing positive human interactions in the various areas of our lives. I, for one, have grown to be particularly interested in EI the moment my now-5-year-old son started preschool. I felt that the pressure to raise a well-adjusted, confident, and admirable boy was more for me, having studied Psychology all my adult life. Learning does not end, does it? And this is why I endeavored to uncover more about the subject as I intend to guide my young son through the intricate web of human emotions as early as I can manage.

The best part of educating myself more about emotional intelligence, beyond being a tenable model to my child, is that I myself am able to improve my own attitude in the relationships I have; I have become more confident in taking on leadership roles at work; and I learned to be more systematic in preserving harmony, even initiating positive changes all around.

There is a multitude of reasons for you to learn and grow along with me. Are you, like me, raising small children? Have you reached a point in your career wherein you feel ready, but are quite hesitant, to take on bigger responsibilities in your career? Do you hit a few similar bumps again and again in your personal relationships that you just can't seem to avoid? If there is even just one "yes" in there, trust me – you should not wait a minute more in acquainting yourself more deeply with your emotional intelligence.

The scientific research you will read in this book will take you steps closer to understanding the variance between individuals with high and low emotional intelligence and on which rung on the EI spectrum you most likely fall. Allow this book to help you become a more self-aware, empathic, and motivated individual. And then witness the unfolding of a better you at the heart of all those you hold dear and true.

The Role of Emotions and How Thoughts and Habits Affect Your Emotions

Emotions play a lead role in emotional intelligence. But what *are* emotions, really? If we are going to be scientific about it, emotions are neural impulses that propel an organism to act as a response to stimuli, both physical and perceived, in its overall need to cope or survive. In other (perhaps simpler) words, emotions are feelings that are expressed through physiological functions such as facial expressions, heart rate, crying, aggressiveness, or self-preservation.

Human emotions are differentiated from the rest of the animal kingdom in that they are pleasant or unpleasant mental states interpreted in the mammalian brain's limbic system. These emotional states are manifested through non-verbal expressions of love, agreement, anger, fear, dislike, sadness, shame, etc. Take love, for instance: it's been theorized as a feeling designed for caring, feeding, and grooming of offsprings originating from a nerve cell network in the brain.

Emotions can be fleeting, such as a flare of irritation with a co-worker, or they can be lingering, such as an enduring sadness from a loss of a loved one. Generally, we can all agree that emotions play a very important role in our thoughts and actions. Our emotions compel us to act in certain ways and influence our decisions greatly.

Emotions are important as they motivate us to take action or make decisions that we hope will bear the best possible impact. Feelings of anxiety over, say an impending exam, pushes us to prepare, study, or rehearse. Likewise, humans are somehow wired to seek social activities or hobbies that will bring forth positive feelings of fulfillment and avoid situations that are potentially boring, stressful, or dangerous.

Emotional health

Getting a better grip of one's emotions is like a series of exercises towards the road to emotional health. People who are said to be "emotionally healthy" are easy to identify: they are individuals who are characteristically aware of their thoughts, feelings, and behaviors. These people have naturally integrated healthy ways to cope with difficulties into their very lifestyles. Problems or stress of any form seem to faze them in no considerable way. Emotionally healthy people generally exude a self-aware and confident air about them and they are highly capable of maintaining positive relationships.

Being emotionally healthy does not mean that you are totally worry-free and are "happy all the time". Having good emotional health means you have a solid grasp of your emotions – you are able to deal with your feelings, whether positive or negative. It is but natural to still have feelings of sadness, anger, stress, and frustration. What distinguishes emotionally healthy people from the rest is that they are able to manage negative feelings of this kind. They can easily tell when a difficulty is more than they are able to handle on their own. Emotionally healthy people do not shirk seeking help, whether professionally or from their trusted support systems.

Our thoughts, then, figure significantly in staying emotionally healthy. Being constantly conscious about your thought processes will greatly impact the train of emotions to actions. Speaking in fitness terms, an honest awareness of your own emotions and how you react make for great "warm-up". Recognize and acknowledge those things in your life that frustrate you, sadden you, and anger you. Address those things by changing them, accepting them, or avoiding them altogether. Not exactly talking about escapism here, but you do not need to seek out the drama, so to speak. Or, in simpler terms: pick your battles. This allows you the ability to express your emotions appropriately. Allow yourself time to think and calm down before doing or saying things you might later regret.

Mayer and Geher, in their study on Emotional Intelligence and the Identification of Emotion, wrote that "people who are good at connecting thoughts to feelings may better 'hear' the emotional implications of their own thoughts, as well as understand the feelings of others from what they say."[1]

With this said, we should all strive to keep our thoughts under control. We might not have total control of the emotion we feel at any given moment. But, by staying focused on our thoughts, we can control our reaction to those emotions. As the saying goes: *"You cannot prevent a bird from landing on your head. But you can keep it from building a nest."*

So, okay, maintaining an objective view of your thoughts as much as possible is crucial in how you interact with everyone else on a daily basis. But how do you make sure your thoughts, as with your emotions, are healthy?

You can stay on top of your thought processes by managing your stress. As much as it is possible, try to change those situations that are typical sources of stress for you. You, of course, will not be able to change everything... so it is ideal if you also strive to learn relaxation techniques that will help you cope. Deep breathing, meditation, exercise, pursuing a talent... there are countless ways to help keep yourself grounded and level-headed in the face of stressors. Find the "sweet spot" between work and play, occupation and rest. Leave time for your hobbies or passions. This healthy balance will help you stay focused on the positive things in your life. You might agree that the beauty of life lies in its imperfections, its unpredictability. Disappointment is inevitable – know how to forgive yourself and others for mistakes. Share this positivity, too, by establishing and harnessing reliable relationships with other people. Humans are social creatures, by nature, and positive connections substantially contribute to one's holistic well-being. Make time for lunch dates and catch-ups; join groups; greet strangers.

Finally – and I can never be more willing to overwork a known cliché right now – take care of your health. Your mental health is hitched on the state of your physical well-being. A mediation analysis was conducted about the relationship between physical and mental health looking at data around direct and indirect effects of past mental health on present physical health and past physical health on present mental health using lifestyle choices and social capital.

> We find significant direct and indirect effects for both forms of health, with indirect effects explaining 10% of the effect of past mental health on physical health and 8% of the effect of past physical health on mental health. Physical activity is the largest contributor to the indirect effects. There are stronger indirect effects for males in mental health (9.9%) and for older age groups in mental health (13.6%) and in physical health (12.6%).[2]

Exercise regularly, eat healthy, and get enough sleep. Do not underestimate the desirable effects of exercise on clarity of the mind. You might have heard about endorphins – hormones secreted by the brain after physical exertion. These neurochemicals interact with the receptors in your brain and reduce the perception of pain. Endorphins also set off a positive feeling in the body, similar to the effects of morphine. But do not abuse substances like drugs or alcohol. These mostly synthetic substances have addictive qualities that inflict harmful effects on the body (not to mention, the mind) with prolonged or excessive use.

Sustain your mind and body with healthy habits. Filling your day-to-day existence with positively-impacting habits will greatly enhance how you perceive situations, conceive your thoughts, understand how you feel, and ultimately, how you express your reactions.

What is Emotional Intelligence

In 1995, renowned psychologist and scientific journalist Daniel Goleman published a book introducing the emerging concept of emotional intelligence to the world. He presented EI as the ability to understand and manage one's emotions which greatly increases one's potential for success and this proposition was welcomed by a world that's growingly thirsty for self-actualization. The concept of emotional intelligence rapidly went on to influence the way people think about emotions and human behavior.

In an article on EI framework published by Salovey and Mayer, emotional intelligence has been defined "as a set of skills hypothesized to contribute to the accurate appraisal and expression of emotion in oneself and in others, the effective regulation of emotion in self and others, and the use of feelings to motivate, plan, and achieve in one's life."[3]

Emotional intelligence refers to how well you are able to manage your emotions, as well as of others'. Amid debates among psychology scholars over what really constitutes emotional intelligence, there is a general agreement that EI consists of at least three skills. These are emotional awareness; the ability to harness one's emotions and leveraging on them in completing tasks such as critical thinking or problem-solving; and the ability to regulate one's own emotions when necessary.

The term "emotional intelligence" (with abbreviations EI or EQ for emotional quotient) was penned by researchers Peter Salavey and John Mayer. The concept was further popularized by Goleman in a book of the same name in 1995. EI is the ability to recognize, understand, and manage one's emotions. EI also includes the ability to recognize and influence the emotions of others. This awareness of our emotions can drive our behavior and can affect people, in both positive and negative ways. This is why learning how to manage emotions – our own and others' – has come to be crucial, most particularly when we are under certain conditions of pressure.

Be aware, though, that EI is an entirely separate principle from Personality. A person's personality is more constant throughout an individual's lifetime, whereas EI is more pliable and can be enhanced, in spite of not being inherently born with it.

In an article by Dr. Travis Bradberry ("Why You Need Emotional Intelligence"), he explained that there have been findings that individuals with average IQs outperform those with the highest IQs 70% of the time. This peculiarity put into question the traditional assumption that intelligence was the sole predictor for success. Years of research now are pointing to a "missing link" – emotional intelligence – which is more critical in setting top performing individuals apart from the rest.

In simpler terms, EI is the "X Factor" ... that "something" intangible in each of us that describes how we manage behavior, how we navigate through complex social intricacies, and how we make decisions that bring about maximum positive returns.

You may have observed, too, that the Top 3 in your highschool class years ago are not necessarily the most successful or the most fulfilled now that you are in your adult lives. You probably know at least one person who was academically outstanding but is socially awkward or possibly frustrated in their careers or personal relationships. One's intelligence quotient (IQ) is not the be-all, end-all indicator of a person's potential for success. Sure, a high IQ might help you get into the college of your choice. But it's your EI that will help you abundantly in managing all the stress and high-level emotions when you are about to take the final exams.

Emotional intelligence is connected to a basic element of human behavior that is separate from intellect. There is no established connection between IQ and EI; these two concepts are in no direct correlation to one another. In other words, how smart someone is will not be indicative of how emotionally intelligent that same person is. Your intelligence is your ability to learn and it is the same when you were 16 as it will be when you're 65. On the other hand, EI is a versatile skill set that can be acquired and improved with consistent practice throughout your life.

Another piece that completes the puzzle that is human behavior is personality. It is the constant "style" that defines a person. An individual's personality hails from his or her genetic preferences, such as the propensity for either extroversion or introversion. Very much like IQ, one's personality is stable and constant throughout his or her lifetime and is not a predictor for emotional intelligence.

The Difference between People with High and Low EI

We have defined emotional intelligence as the ability to recognize, understand, and manage emotions. This extends to the ability to recognize and influence the emotions of others around us. The level of awareness of our own emotions drive how we behave and eventually affect people, whether positively or negatively.

In our endless attempts at understanding those who we interact with, viewing someone from the EI perspective makes getting to know them easier. How do you tell if a person has high EI? What are the indications of low EI in a person?

Low emotional intelligence negatively impacts most, if not all, areas of any person's life. There will often be a certain awkwardness in school, work, family, friendships, even in romantic relationships. A lot of a low EI person's relationships will often feel strained or problematic.

An emotionally intelligent person is keenly in touch with his emotions, including frustration, sadness, and all else unpleasant. He or she has no difficulty identifying the emotion, thus managing it is nearly effortless as well. People with high EI are just as in tune to the emotions of others. This sensitivity to emotions, both of the self and of others, renders these people as better partners, friends, parents, and leaders.

If you think that your emotional skills could use a little work, or if you believe you have the makings of a healthy EI, the good news is that these abilities can be assimilated and, yes... enhanced.

Below are a few more specific characteristics of individuals with high EI:

You ponder on feelings. The first indicator of emotional intelligence is awareness – both of the self and of the society in which you belong. With this, you are able to recognize emotions and their impact on yourself and on others. This kind of awareness stems from frequent reflection. You ask yourself questions like:

- What are my strengths, emotionally? Where am I weakest?
- In what ways do my moods affect my thoughts and decisions?

- What might be going on beneath the surface causing (another person) to behave that way?

Reflecting on questions like these puts you at an advantage in regulating your behavior and influencing others' as well.

You appreciate the "power" of the pause. You have no trouble taking a thoughtful moment before you speak or act, especially in complicated or charged situations. You know how important it is to calculate your moves in order to avoid embarrassing moments or making commitments hastily. Simply put, pausing helps you avoid making irreversible decisions based on momentary emotions.

You take criticism constructively. Typically, people dread negative feedback. But you believe that criticism is a valuable learning opportunity. And even when criticism appears baseless, you still accept this as a helpful preview to how others might perceive you. For you, criticism always brings you to ask yourself: *"How can this help me be better?"*

You operate with genuineness or sincerity. Sincerity is not necessarily about always sharing everything about you to everyone. This genuineness is about staying loyal to your values and principles, saying what you mean, and meaning what you say. It's true, not everyone will welcome what you have to say. What's important is that you are true and the ones who actually matter will appreciate you more for it.

You are empathic. You are connected with others through thoughts and feelings. You do not judge or label people; instead, you try to view things from their perspective. You understand that empathy does not mean that you agree with another person's point of view. Empathy is about your natural willingness to understand their position.

You are quick to praise. It is human nature to crave recognition or appreciation. You are always focused on the good in others. When you are generous with sincere praises, this helps build trust that you are an objective, selfless individual. This inspires others to work harder and always aim to reach their full potential.

You are able to give meaningful feedback. You are perfectly able to frame criticism as constructive feedback. This is because you know that criticism comes with the possibility of being offensive to some. You always strive to be helpful rather than harmful.

You apologize. You possess the humility that gives you courage to easily seek forgiveness whenever you know that you've committed errors. This humility will allow others to trust you better. An emotionally intelligent person believes that apologizing is more about valuing relationships above one's own self-esteem.

You are forgiving. You have fully realized that holding on to resentment is like leaving a bullet inside a gunshot wound, preventing any kind of absolute healing. While he or she who has offended you may have moved on with his or her life, harboring resentment is like denying yourself the opportunity to fully heal. When you forgive, you let go of residual hurt and free yourself from any form of emotional hold by those who do not deserve it. You know that this is the only way to move forward.

You keep your promises. Nowadays, it is easy for a lot of people to just skip on commitments for, sometimes, the flimsiest of reasons. An emotionally intelligent person has made a habit of keeping his word. In things both big and small, you endeavor to keep your promises. This proves to everyone that you are reliable and trustworthy.

You are altruistic. You possess a genuine selfless concern for others. The best way to make a positive impact on others is to help them. You know that a person's real worth is not measured by his college degrees or career accomplishments. What turns you into a true person of substance has more to do with the amount of time he you devote to helping others. Being sincerely altruistic influences others to trust you and follow your generous lead.

You defend yourself against emotional sabotage. So, yes, emotional intelligence is the ability to recognize and manage the emotions of others as well as your own. Herein lies the dark side of EI: some people might attempt to manipulate others to their detriment for some selfish cause. And this is one of the reasons why you continue to exercise your own emotional intelligence: it is so you can protect yourself from self-serving attempts like these from others.

On the other end of the spectrum, you can detect a person with low EI if he or she is:

Frequently getting into arguments. Individuals with low EI are somehow challenged in their understanding of the emotions of others and this difficulty often finds them getting

25

into arguments. People with opportunities for emotional intelligence seem to easily get embroiled in heated disagreements with friends, family, co-workers, and even random strangers. Their inability to manage their emotions well together with a disconnect from other people's emotions cause them to instinctively construe disagreement as heated conflict.

Unable to interpret how others feel. Low EI individuals are typically oblivious (or "dense", in popular speak) to other people's feelings. They do not seem to "get" when other people are angry with or dislike them. Worse, people with low EI would always resent why others seem to expect him or her to know how they are feeling. Emotions, in general, can be quite exasperating for low EI individuals.

Unable to cope with highly emotional situations. Related to the previous characteristic, the exasperation over emotions that low EI individuals feel results to an inability to cope with strong emotions. In other words, emotions, both their own or others', are hard to understand, much less deal with. A low EI individual would typically just walk away from highly emotional situations. Concealing their true feelings is also typical for low EI individuals.

Quick to dismiss other people as "too sensitive". People with low EI seem to perceive emotional signals inaccurately. This is why it may be typical for them to be cracking jokes at the most inopportune times. And when the other people around convey a certain annoyance or dislike for these inappropriate jokes or comments, the low EI individual would always dismiss them as simply being overly sensitive.

Lacks empathy. It then comes as no surprise that someone with an inability to understand other people's emotions would have little to no empathy for others. It would, of course, be impossible for a low EI individual to "put himself in another person's shoes" since he does not get what that other person is feeling to begin with.

Close-minded to other points of view. To a low EI person, he or she is always right. They will always vigorously defend their position and refuse to consider what other people have to say, especially if it negates their own views. A low EI person is often pessimistic and hyper-critical of other people's emotions.

Quick to blame others for mistakes. When things go wrong, people with low EI would instinctively blame others. They would typically attribute the error of their own actions to the conditions of the situation or to the behavior of others, other than owning up to it. To their mind, they were forced into error by external factors and all the others are just not understanding their situation. This refusal to take responsibility thus often leaves them feeling bitter or victimized.

Prone to emotional outbursts. A low EI person's inability to understand and manage his or her emotions render him or her prone to unexpected emotional outbursts. These outbursts would typically be uncontrollable or overwrought.

Has difficulty keeping friendships. At the end of the day, with all this awkwardness in social situations earlier described, low EI individuals will show a difficulty in maintaining friendships. Deep and meaningful friendships require a "give-and-take" dynamic when it comes to feelings, compassion, and support. All these would be a struggle for someone with low EI.

Existing EI Models

After years of research since its introduction by Salovey, Mayer, and Goleman during the early 1990's, emotional intelligence has been the subject of substantial empirical study. The continuously growing interest in EI has produced an enormous store of resources that scholars have invested in throughout years of studying the concept of EI, which, in turn, has led to vast amounts of models, instruments and investigations on the subject. In the hopes of standardizing literature on EI, Joseph and Newman[4] proposed three EI models -- distinguished primarily by the types of measuring instruments utilized.

Ability Model

The Ability Model of EI was developed by researchers Peter Salovey and John Mayer. In this model, EI is regarded as a form of intelligence that is based on an individual's emotional aptitudes, and is viewed as a mental ability that involves reasoning about one's emotions. This model focuses on how an individual perceives and understands his and others' emotions by way of nonverbal cues such as facial expressions or body language. It measures EI abilities in terms of critical thinking or cognitive activities using emotions as basis. The Ability Model measures EI in terms of how a person attempts to interpret the emotions of others and his ability to recognize the target of emotions more accurately. For instance, being able to detect if the emotion of anger is being directed at the individual or at the surrounding situation.

Within this model, a person's EI is evaluated by how one solves emotional problems through performance tests with prescribed sets of correct and incorrect responses. The instrument that is most representative of this model is known as the "Mayer-Salovey-Caruso Emotional Intelligence Test" (MSCEIT; Mayer et al.).[5]

Trait Model

The Trait Model of EI was developed by Konstantin Vasily Petrides. Petrides defines this model as "a constellation of emotional self-perceptions located at the lower levels of personality." This model takes a look at an individual's understanding of his or her own emotions. In this model, EI is seen as an individual's self-perceptions of their own emotions, behavior, and other abilities. It utilizes the personality framework in investigating trait emotional intelligence. Similar to the Ability Model, the Trait model views EI as a combination of emotional aptitudes. Just that, in this model, self-report instruments are used for measurement, wherein participants must estimate their own EI in a subjective manner. In this approach, the "Trait Meta-Mood Scale" (TMMS; Salovey et al.)[6] is a widely used instrument.

Mixed Model

David Goleman's Mixed Model does not classify EI as a form of intelligence and instead considers it as a broad concept that encompasses "The Five Elements" to efficiently define EI. These five elements are believed to be:

1. Self-Awareness (the ability to recognize one's own emotions)
2. Self-Regulation (the ability for self-control, trustworthiness, adaptability)
3. Motivation (a person's drive, commitment, initiative, optimism)
4. Empathy (the ability to understand others's feelings, acceptance of diversity, political awareness)
5. Social Skills (one's leadership, conflict management, communication skills)

As with the previous models, the Mixed Model utilizes self-report instruments that measure the subjective perception of the participant. The most common test for the Mixed Model is the "Bar-On Emotional Quotient Inventory (EQi)", named after its creator Reuven Bar-On.[7] This instrument is a self-report measure of emotional and social intelligence that estimates a participant's emotional quotient.

Despite the variations across these three models, their use has yielded a significant number of findings related to the study of emotional intelligence. A noteworthy example is this:

> "Researchers have linked higher EI scores to better mental and physical health (Schutte et. al.[8]; Martins et. al.[9]; Zeidner et. al.[10]), well-being and happiness (Cabello and Fernández-Berrocal[11]; Sánchez-Álvarez et. al.[12]), job performance (Côté[13]), prosocial behavior (Mavroveli et. al.[14]), less aggressive behavior (García-Sancho et. al.[15]), and substance abuse (Kun and Demetrovics[16])."[17]

Elements of Emotional Intelligence (Mixed Model by Goleman)

One of the most popular models of EI was developed by Daniel Goleman. The Mixed Model of EI focuses mainly on studying EI through the individuals' skills and competencies that affect performance in leadership roles. This is why Goleman's model of EI is typical in corporate and other professional settings. Goleman's Mixed Model of EI is highly suitable in the training and evaluation of individuals showing high potential for management roles.

Goleman's Mixed Model proposes that there are five important elements to Emotional Intelligence. Within each element of EI in the Mixed Model, Goleman outlined a set of emotional abilities which are now referred to as "hallmarks". These qualities are not a person's innate talents or personality characteristics, but rather capabilities that can be learned and enhanced to achieve heightened levels of performance. These five elements are:

Self-Awareness

Your self-awareness is your ability to recognize your own emotions, strengths and weaknesses, goals, what motivates you, and your values. This also includes your ability to recognize your effect on others; particularly how intuitive you are when it comes to influencing the emotions of others around you.

Definitive indications of your self-awareness would be your level of self-confidence, your most objective assessments of yourself, and your abilities for self-deprecating sense of humor.

Your self-awareness relies on your ability to monitor your own emotions and how accurately you are able to identify others' emotions.

Self-Regulation

Your ability for self-regulation involves how you recognize your own disruptive emotions (including your impulses) and how you control or channel these negative emotions to a more productive direction. How well do you think before you act and are you able to suspend judgment for later?

The hallmarks for your ability to self-regulate include your levels of trustworthiness and integrity, how comfortable you are with uncertainty, and how you embrace change.

Motivation

How you are able to motivate yourself towards the successful achievement of your own goals speaks to your own emotional intelligence, according to the Mixed Model. This includes both your practical goals (such as a raise or promotion at work) and your drive for achievement, per se. The Mixed Model is outlined to identify highly emotionally intelligent individuals who strive for success just for the sake of, well… succeeding.

Are you driven more by external rewards (such as money and status), or are you motivated by the more meaningful things in life such as joy, a natural desire to learn, or by the inward fulfillment that comes from being charitable? How persistent are you in pursuing these goals of yours?

The hallmarks of motivation would be how strong your drive to achieve is, your optimism in the face of defeat, and your commitment to the organizations you belong in.

Empathy

Empathy, in general terms, is your ability to understand and share in the feelings of others. Not to be confused with sympathy, which is feeling sorry for another person experiencing difficulties, empathy is more about being able to personally identify with the experience (or experiences) of another and taking the shared emotion into consideration in deciding how to relate to that other person.

How well do you understand the emotional makeup of others? Are you always able to treat other people appropriately, given their emotional states?

In the workplace, the hallmarks of empathy include expertise in developing and retaining talent, cultural sensitivity, and service to clients and customers. In the more generic context, empathy is often thought to encroach on, or lead to, sympathy, which involves concern or a desire to mitigate negative emotions or experiences in others. Take note, however, that empathy is not necessarily equivalent to compassion. Empathy can be employed for either compassionate or cruel behavior. Take, for instance, serial rapists who are able to attract only to eventually violate several partners -- they tend to have great empathic skills. Otherwise, they would not have been able to draw victims close so easily.

Social Skills

This element of EI rides heavily on your abilities for self-awareness and self-regulation in the realm of your relationships with others. Are you able to persuade others into the direction you wish them to go? If you manage people at work, how creative are you in motivating your team members? In personal relationships, how well do you communicate your positive attributes and keep your friends or partner interested in being around you?

Are you able to manage your existing relationships without difficulty? Are you able to build rapport with others without much effort? The hallmarks of social skills are effectiveness in initiating change, persuasiveness, and the ability to build and lead a group.

The Mixed Model concurs that people are born with cognitive abilities and personality characteristics. And these inherent traits, unique to each individual, are highly instrumental in determining a person's potential for success when coupled with an active development of his or her emotional intelligence.

This is mainly why the Mixed Model of EI is highly popular in the business setting. Business organizations find the theories related to EI to be quite effective in maximizing their human resources. It is not uncommon for manpower-rich business organizations to perform evaluations of existing staff members or potential hires based on the Mixed Model's set of values. Gauging the EI levels of potential hires as early as in the recruitment stages and further developing current staff's EI will only serve any business' culture and, yes, bottom line well.

How Emotional Intelligence Looks Like in Action

When it comes to achieving professional success, mutually beneficial personal relationships, and self-actualization, EI is just as important as your intellectual abilities. Most of the time, probably even more.

Individuals with high EI find it easier to build and keep very solid relationships, constantly succeed at work, and ultimately to feel great about themselves for being the kind of person they can actually admire.

Highly emotionally intelligent people, in a nutshell, are able to recognise their own emotional states as well as the emotional states of others. Thus, they are able to engage with people in ways that draw them closer. Anybody can practice, develop, and utilize the ability to understand emotions so as to be able to relate better to other people, form healthier relationships, come out (and stay!) ahead at work... generally leading a more enriched and fulfilling life, all in all.

In Leadership Roles and Career

Emotional intelligence, as we all should understand by now, is a person's ability to recognize, understand, and manage emotions. Possessing this ability is critical to interpersonal communication, which, in turn, is highly essential every person's personal and professional relationships.

Interest in the psychology of emotions and the then new concept of emotional intelligence truly caught on with the 1995 publication of the book *Emotional Intelligence: Why it can Matter More Than IQ* written by Daniel Goleman. In this celebrated book, Goleman put forth that EI is possibly just as important, if not more so, in predicting a person's success in life. These emotional skills, Goleman argued, thus plays a significantly important role in the workplace.

The next logical question would then be: How much impact does EI have on your professional success? As EI is studied and understood more and more through the years, it becomes increasingly apparent that EI contributes abundantly in a person's potential for success at work. Emotional intelligence is any individual's potent guide in navigating the social complexities of the workplace. Likewise, a person's EI allows him to effectively lead and motivate others, therefore exponentially increasing his or her potentials in excelling in his or her chosen career. This is why EI assessment tools have come to be an integral part of countless business organizations' hiring processes, together with the pertinent tests for technical abilities.

A known EI resource entity, TalentSmart, tested EI paralleled with 33 workplace competencies and found that EI is the strongest predictor of an employee's performance, with data that support the 58% success rate in different job types.

Other studies conducted in workplace settings have revealed that about 90% of top-performing individuals scored high in EI. Of course, there was a number of low-performing employees who scored high in EI, too, but this figure is not more than 20%. It is possible, yes, to be a top performer at work while one lacks in EI, but this is unlikely.

It is nearly a given that high EI people make more, salary-wise. High EI employees generally make an average, per year, of $29,000 more than people with low EI scores. Research data showed a direct correlation between EI and earnings in that every EI point increase adds about $1,300 to the annual salary.[18]

These findings apply to workers across all industries, all job levels, in every region across the globe. TalentSmart stated that, after substantial research data and analysis, they have not yet identified a job in which performance and compensation are not closely linked to EI.

Staffing solutions specialist Career Builder conducted a survey among hiring managers and found that close to 75% of survey respondents indicated that an employee's EI is more valuable to the organization than IQ.[19]

EI is valued by business organizations because of these consistently observed positive behavior in the workplace:

EI gives the person the ability to make better business decisions. Because the high EI individual is self-aware and in tune with the feelings of others, he or she is highly capable of coming up with decisions that are beneficial to the greater number.

Highly emotionally intelligent employees are more capable of keeping their composure under pressure.

Because highly emotional situations rarely faze them, they are able to maintain calm in the face of challenges.

Relatedly, high EI allows for effectivity in conflict resolution. Their assured demeanor comes highly advantageous to emotionally charged scenarios.

High EI individuals in leadership roles display more empathy. As such, they are able to lead by example.

High EI employees respond to criticism well. They have no difficulty listening, reflecting, and positively responding to negative feedback. To these individuals, negative feedback is still constructive.

There is, thus, no wonder why EI is a widely recognized and highly valued skill in the workplace where business decisions and relationships rely heavily on interpersonal communication, understanding, and teamwork. The good news for all of us is that researchers believe any person's EI can be improved with training and practice. While emotional skills may be inherent to some people, there are things that we can do to help improve our abilities to understand and reason with our emotions. As with others'.

How well do you communicate with others? Do you find yourself frequently impatient, easily annoyed, or quick to anger? What are some ways you can deal with these feelings effectively? Make it a habit to examine yourself in order to recognize your strengths and weaknesses.This type of candid, inward reflection will only serve you well as you look for ways to enrich yourself further or deal with your shortcomings.

Stay alert to the wave of emotions that come at you throughout the day. How do these emotions trigger you and how do you respond? Do your emotions impact how you make decisions or the quality of your interaction with others? Pay attention to your own emotions and how they figure in your everyday life at work. And should you realize that you are somehow wanting in your responses to particular emotions, make it a point to remember that emotions are typically and characteristically fleeting and can be highly volatile. It is not unusual to be irritated with a co-worker or your boss assigning you a task that frustrates you. Before you express any reaction, keep in mind that these feelings are temporary, and so making decisions hastily based on the heat of momentary emotions can negatively impact your progress, goals, and success.

Read up on techniques that may be helpful to you in dealing with stress in the workplace. Establishing and keeping hobbies entirely separated from work is a good start. Physical exercise is usually a healthy channel to release stress. When you are able to manage your stress, you are more capable of taking time to think before making decisions. Emotions can be overwhelming, at times, and no one should be making definite decisions while under the influence of intense emotions. You will be able to make decisions you can live with if you've had time to consider all possibilities objectively.

Make it a point to listen to what others have to say. Not in a passive or indifferent way, that you will never interrupt. Being an active listener conveys that you are passionate about work projects and are willing to work with others for the company's greater good. Active listening entails paying attention to non-verbal cues in communication. The signals that people send through body language, tone, and facial expression indicate a lot about what they truly think or believe.

Be the kind of employee that avoids office drama, but make sure you know what to do in times of unavoidable conflict. As much as you can help it, stay as far away from office politicking that are typical for most workplaces. Focusing on what everyone else has to say and aiming to find the best solution to the difficulty contributes a lot to managing tension.

Notice how you respond to others. Do you give others ample opportunities to share their ideas? Do you acknowledge their input, even if you don't agree with them? Assuring the people that you work with that their efforts have substance and bearing often helps everyone become more open to compromise. This is always a healthy culture to cultivate in any organization. Do not be quick in dismissing ideas you disagree with, and instead try to view the idea from the other party's perspective. Yes, this is not very easy, especially when the idea appears weak on all fronts. But rather than allowing disagreements to balloon into major struggles, spend time looking at the situation from your peer's or subordinate's perspective. Doing so is a great first step toward finding a middle ground between two opposing points of view.

Do everything you can to maintain a positive attitude. Optimistic people in the workplace are highly effective in inspiring and motivating others. More than that, you will be able to keep a positive attitude toward your own work and thus become more productive. Focus on all the things that you love about your job. No job is perfect; there will always be upsides and downsides. Instead of dwelling on your challenges, motivate yourself by focusing on the aspects of your job that you most enjoy. Do you love the feeling of accomplishment you get when you complete a major initiative? Or maybe there is fulfillment from helping your trainees progress toward their own goals? No matter what it is, identify those elements in your job and draw inspiration from them.

EI is not a competency reserved only for the CEOs and the senior leadership team. EI is a quality that is vital at each and every level of any person's career, whether one is a college student seeking an internship or a seasoned employee vying for a leadership role. If you wish to be effective in your job and successfully move up the career ladder, never forget that emotional intelligence is critical to achieving your goals.

In Relationships

Emotional intelligence is just as, if not more, essential in personal relationships as it is in the workplace.

You could be striving to become a more sympathetic spouse, an indispensable BFF, or a "cool-as-a-monk" patient parent. Whatever your aspirations are in terms of your personal relationships, EI can transform your relationships for the better. Even if you haven't always been the most emotionally available partner, friend, or parent in the past, the great thing about EI is that it's never too late to start.

Happily married couples aren't those that are prettier, richer, or more mentally astute than others. It's those who have discovered a dynamic that keeps the negative from overwhelming the positive that's more joyful in their married lives. It is only natural for two people in a marriage, who live under the same roof, come home to each other after every long day, to feel negative emotions toward each other at certain points. What keeps them together is not allowing these negative feelings cancel out the best ones. This is called an emotionally intelligent marriage.

The higher the EI of two people involved in a marriage (or any relationship, for that matter) the more capable they are to understand, respect, and honor each other. Happily ever after, so to speak.

A husband that possesses a high EI is characteristically always interested in his wife's emotions. An emotionally intelligent husband has no difficulties in honoring and respecting his wife. While he may not express his emotions in the same way his wife does, a high EI husband will want to learn how to better connect with his wife. It is typical for a husband who lacks EI to reject his wife's influence because he fears losing power or control. And this unwillingness to accept influence renders him to be uninfluential as well.

Highly emotional intelligent individuals are well capable of resolving emotional conflicts appropriately and promptly. These people are able to accurately perceive emotions from other people's faces. They would easily know, for instance, that angry people can be dangerous, that happiness means that someone will welcome company, and that some sad or fearful people may prefer to be left alone. High EI people also know how to manage their own and others' emotions. They have realized, for example, that sadness can be conducive for analytical thought and so they may prefer to reflect when they are in a somber mood.[20]

While the ability to read other people's emotions is essential for healthy EI, the ability to understand and express your own emotions is just as important. If you believe yourself to be generally keen about other people's emotions, yet cannot seem to understand the shifts in mood or emotional responses of your partner, it is possible that he or she is missing the key element of EI.

It is basic that a great deal of emotion is communicated through a person's tone of voice. If your friend, spouse, co-worker, child, or relative cannot seem to sense your irritation or joy from the sound and tone of your voice, this is because this other person is unable to detect emotion in others.

If you are in a relationship with someone who cannot seem to read your real feelings at any given time, expect that this other person will have difficulties in establishing emotional connections with you or others. This inability to comprehend emotions – both his and others' – will, of course result to a failure to respond appropriately in most situations. This particular challenge will, of course, result to difficulties in making, or even keeping, good relationships. This is a glaring indication of low EI.

We've learned that emotionally intelligent individuals are able to identify and regulate their own emotions. They are able to easily acknowledge whenever they are frustrated, sad, or angry. This ability to control one's emotions *does not* mean bottling it up inside or brushing it aside. It means that once you have identified your emotion and likely its source, you are able to pause accordingly before expressing any definitive reaction which you might later regret. This ability to regulate emotions also means being able to remain steadfast and "being there" for, say a sibling when a parent is diagnosed with a life-threatening disease, in spite of the fact that you share the same anxiety or sadness. If a person you know is prone to lashing out in rage, dwells in loneliness for an unreasonably long time or gets extra giddy over the slightest of provocations, then it is likely that this person is lacking in EI.

People with high EI understand that their thoughts give birth to their emotions, and so they make it a point to remain objective in controlling their trains of thought. This is why they are able to "water down" their emotions and sanitize their reactions. They are aware that their moods and certain external stimulation can greatly affect thoughts, and so people with high EI are characteristically calm in the face of conflict and know to put off making decisions when they are upset.

You would know if you have high EI if you understand the connection between your actions to how other people react emotionally. You are able to admit accountability because you are open to other people's perspectives. In example, you know that if you break a promise, this will likely elicit hurt or disappointment in the other person and you will never blame the other person for being "too sensitive". Empathy and sympathy are likewise definite indicators of EI. Your ability to recognize the emotional state of others allows you to reflect back the appropriate emotional response.

For any relationship to stay healthy, the individuals involved need to flourish together. This entails learning what the other person loves about you, including those things that he or she thinks you could stand to improve. An emotionally intelligent person, or someone who is still striving to improve on his or her emotional skills, would easily accept feedback and effect the necessary changes. This, without having to resort to resentment or other defensive behaviors.

Further than this, knowing what your partner needs before they actually ask can serve you well in any relationship, whether you're providing a shoulder to cry on or ordering a favorite dumpling off the Chinese takeout menu on your way home from work. Emotionally intelligent people are virtually effortless in this ability.

"EQ helps you predict your loved one's needs and wants more accurately," says Dr. Inna Khazan, PhD. "You will be more likely to get just the right gift or say just the right thing to comfort them when they are having a hard time."[21]

If you wish to be the kind of person that your significant other, friend, colleague, or child always opens up to, start by seriously and sincerely reflecting on your own levels of EI. Being emotionally intelligent requires that you are in touch with your emotional needs as well as with theirs. This makes it significantly easier for them to come to you when they are longing for guidance, support, or even just pleasant company. With work and various other commitments eating time off from your relationship, it's sometimes easy to lose focus and veer away from the life you've envisioned with the one you're in a relationship with. Exercising your EI makes it easier for you to recognize what you truly value, thus it will seem effortless to carve out the time and prioritize the feelings of this other person you are in a relationship with.

When he or she needs to talk, you will put your smart phone down and listen. You always think in "we" terms rather than just "me". An emotionally intelligent partner or friend always desires to understand the other person's inner self and will show respect by focusing on him or her. A person who is constantly aiming to hone his or her emotional abilities will simply have a better quality of life than the person who neglects his or her EI.

Especially in romantic relationships, being an active listener can actually spell the difference between "the long haul" and "this is not working". In fact, studies have shown that people whose partners were good listeners had better emotional states and less stress-related physical infirmities. If you are in a relationship with someone who is in tune with your emotions and is understanding of your emotional needs, then you can count yourself lucky. Reciprocate this level of emotional intelligence by being an active, receptive listener yourself.

Bear in mind that the one true constant in relationships (actually, life) is change. Throughout your lifetime, you are bound to change jobs or careers, homes, mentors, hairstyles, etc. An emotionally intelligent relationship partner is able to anticipate and understand these changes and how it affects the both of you and the actual relationship. People with high EI are great at embracing change rather than rejecting it.

Even worse than changes, every kind of relationship is bound to hit a few bumps now and then – most of them, neither of you will see coming. While it is easier for some to flee in the face of challenges, highly emotionally intelligent people will already have realized that weathering the storm and making the relationship work is worth the bumpy ride together.

And staying emotionally intelligent throughout the storms in your relationship only helps you see the goodness in each other. The tricky part to long-time relationships is that people may fall into the usual trap of taking his or her partner for granted at some point. This will not be a problem for a partner with high EI. For someone who has above-average EI, he or she will be able to tell when he or she has not been showing appreciation as much as he or she should. Catching this on time allows the high EI partner to correct the behavior and remedy the weakness. Also, EI helps one distinguish behaviors of unintentional detachment, rather than hastily assuming that the other is acting out of deliberate attempt to offend. In other words, EI allows you to afford your partner the benefit of the doubt in times of uncertainty.

In summary, by understanding your own emotions and learning to control them, you will be a natural in expressing what you feel exactly and understanding how others are feeling. This enables you to communicate more effectively and sincerely, ensuring that you are a genuine candidate for long-term healthy relationships, whether at work or at home.

In Your Personal Development

On a more personal level, EI is the "something" in each of us. Though intangible and sometimes seemingly abstract, it greatly affects how we manage our behavior, make our way through and around social complexities, and make personal decisions that yield positive results.

If you are serious about being "all that you can be", building your EI is an inevitable task. It can be quite tough at the start, sure, but as you become more and more attuned to your emotions, things will begin to feel very natural for you. One of the best ways to begin developing your EI is to observe your thoughts. Examine how your thoughts link to your emotions all throughout your day. Various studies have seen that our thoughts help trigger certain chemicals in the brain that contribute to our emotions[22]. Establish the connection between the succession of your activities or thoughts and the ensuing feelings. Look for possible patterns. Once you recognize any pattern, you can begin working toward diminishing your negative emotions. Simultaneously, you are able to identify thoughts that result to positive feelings. Then, you'll know which thoughts (or thought-provoking activities) to avoid and which to harness.

What calms your nerves? Is it a long walk, a 5K run, or getting on the phone with your friends? Yoga is a hugely popular wellness exercise these days. Figure out what activities provoke your best thoughts and strive to do more of them as much as you can.

Unfortunately, none of us can ever escape a difficult or negative person in our daily encounters. If there is someone like this who is a constant in your life (perhaps at home, work, school, or in your neighborhood), strive to be proactively positive whenever you need to interact with him or her. Before actually striking up a conversation with people like this, make a mental note of the positives that could be derived from talking with them. Focus on those, instead of coming into contact with a default dread or dislike. Also make sure that you are in a positive place at that instant, too, before attempting to connect so you will not be easily drawn into a negative place during the contact.

Practice reading other people's emotions. This can be tricky, especially with people who are characteristically stoic or not very emotionally expressive. Of course it will be easy to tell when someone is sad when they are uncommonly quiet or crying. But can you tell when someone is feeling down but is trying to hide it? People with high EI can distinguish this and, with conscious effort and practice, you can, too.

Build up on your emotional vocabulary. We all experience emotions, but not all of us are able to accurately identify these feelings as they happen. Research shows that only 36% of people are able to successfully identify emotions[23], which is unfortunate because un- or mis- labeled emotions are likely to be misunderstood. This is highly rife for irrational choices and, sometimes, counterproductive behavior. People with high EI are able to understand their emotions and an extensive vocabulary of emotions only help them to do so. While many people might describe themselves as simply feeling "bad," emotionally intelligent people will be more succinct in describing themselves as "irritable", "frustrated", "anxious", or "exasperated". The more specific your definition for your emotion is, the better you can understand the situation, what caused it, and what you should do about it.

Be persistently positive. These days, simply watching the evening news can make it quite impossible to stay positive. What with all the never-ending war, violence, volatile economies, natural disasters, disease, etc., right? The whole world may seem to be working double time toward its self-destruction… but an emotionally intelligent person will not dwell in worry because it is in their character to not allow themselves be caught up in things that they cannot control. Instead, people with high EI focus their energies on the two things that actually *are* in their power to control: their attention and behavior. Certain studies have found that optimistic people are generally more physiologically and psychologically healthier than people of pessimistic nature. Naturally, it's the optimists who perform better in their jobs and have richer relationships. Keep this in mind so you are able to arrest negative thoughts before they overwhelm you.

Bring happiness to everything you do. People with high EI easily know what causes them joy and they are proactive in bringing happiness in everything they do. Try, whenever possible, to turn monotonous work into creative and fun games. Take the extra step in making those that you care about happy. Fight the "war against stress" for as many people as you are able to. Be the advocate of resilience and motivate others along the way.

Be politely assertive. High EI individuals are able to balance propriety, empathy, and kindness with their ability to assert themselves and initiate boundaries. This tactful character is extremely ideal for handling conflicts. Most people, when they are offended, default to passive or aggressive behavior. Highly emotionally intelligent people, on the other hand, keep their balance and remain assertive; they veer away from any kind of unfiltered emotional reaction. This allows them the ability to neutralize difficult or "toxic" people without making enemies out of them.

Keep your curiosity about other people. Regardless if you are an introvert of if you're an extrovert, maintain a healthy curiosity about everyone around you. Emotionally intelligent people have this curiosity as a by-product of their ability to empathize, another significant hallmark of high EI. The more one cares about other people and what they are going through, the more curiosity one is bound to have about them.

Forgive, but don't forget. Emotionally intelligent people adhere to the time-honored motto "fool me once, shame on you; fool me twice, shame on me." Forgive, so as to forego grudges. People with high EI realize that holding on to grudges can be stressful and can have ill consequences to one's well-being. So you should learn how to forgive. But you need not forget. You should not offer up chances to your wrong-doers to hurt you once more. Emotionally intelligent people will never allow themselves to be held down by mistreatment, so they quickly let go of grudges but stay assertive in protecting themselves from any more future harm.

Be difficult to offend. Make it hard for others to hurt you. You can do so by keeping a firm grasp of who you truly are. When you have a solid knowing of yourself, others' words or actions cannot easily offend you. People with high EI are self-confident and open-minded, thus are not overly or unreasonably sensitive.

Stop demeaning self-talk. Do not empower your negative thoughts by allowing them to "marinate" inside you. Tell yourself that most of your negative thoughts are exactly just that: thoughts. They are not necessarily factual. An effective technique is to listen to your inner voice when it starts to say negative things… and write them down. This exercise slows down the negative momentum and allows you to clear your head and rationally evaluate the truth in these negative thoughts. One indication of exaggeration is the use of superlatives like "never", "ever", "worst" and the like. Once on paper and you feel that a negative statement sounds factual, seek a trusted friend's advice and ask if he or she agrees with this thought of yours. Third party insight plus your own usually adds up to the truth.

Unlike one's intelligence, EI is thoroughly pliable. As you consistently "train" your mind by repeatedly practicing emotionally intelligent behavior, your brain builds pathways toward turning these practices into habits. Persistently work at this and it won't take long before you begin to naturally respond to everyone around you with such intelligence, emotionally. And as your brain reinforces these new positive behaviors, you will find that the old destructive behaviors will just die of natural causes.

Take Action: Improving your EI

If you are reading this book to learn more about EI, chances are high that you are likewise desiring to improve this in you. After all, the ability to identify, understand, and manage emotions – both yours and others' – can only lead you to heights of success, both at work and at home.

If you are managing a business, say in the service industry, you'll need a wide skill set to attract and satisfy customers. If you are a head of a household, you need to deal with different personalities day in and day out. It can happen that a single miscalculation or lapse in interaction can cause a drastic or irreversible change, turning your customer satisfaction or home dynamic from good to bad. While a variety of factors contribute to the success of a business or domestic harmony, there is always one quality that makes a difference: emotional intelligence.

EI has been revealed to be THAT intangible factor that predicts the likelihood of success in all fronts: at work, in your personal relationships, and in your growth as a desirable individual. EI, being the valuable ability to perceive and manage emotions both of the self and of others', has become a critical element in hiring and recruitment processes in countless business organizations. Likewise, people in all kinds of relationships are realizing the important role of emotional acuity in any enduring relationship.

Generally, EI, as a facet of human behavior, is divided into four spheres of emotional competencies, with self-awareness being the first and perhaps most important quality. Self-awareness is one's ability to identify his or her own emotions and understand how these emotions affect any given situation. If you have a healthy self-awareness, you are able to deal with problems and address complications as they surface. This trait will certainly be beneficial to all those present in the different facets of your life – whether you are wearing your professional "hat" and interacting with colleagues or you are with your family or friends and directing your personal dynamics.

The next sphere of EI is self-regulation. Know that without this ability to control your own emotions, your self-awareness is not going to count for much. Self-regulation allows you to keep your impulses and emotions in check. This trait is especially important for parents, romantic partners, and if you are managing people in a work setting. You might have already experienced letting your emotions get the best of you. Would you agree with me when I say that emotional blowouts don't always look pretty, especially in after-thought? Have you ever felt, after the adrenaline has ebbed, that you could've handled the situation better? The ability to adapt to ever-changing conditions while keeping your emotions under control bestows upon you a certain power or authority, with the people you interact with learning to trust you to be the most ideal person to settle disputes or help sort out misunderstandings.

The third sphere is social awareness. This is the ability to identify and understand the emotions of others, allowing you a certain advantage at influencing their emotions and, sometimes, ensuing decisions. A thriving social awareness also renders you to be resilient to change, thus able to model motivating actions among those around you.

Your level of social awareness likewise affords you the ability to better empathize and connect with others. Empathy is EI's fourth sphere. Are you able to read and understand the emotional structure of other people? If you are, then you are likely always able to treat other people appropriately, according to their emotional states.

Professionals and personal partners with high EI are able to navigate social situations more adeptly, are able to understand other people's moods and behaviors, and are good at responding appropriately in most, if not all, situations. Therefore, they are often in better positions to succeed compared to everybody else.

If you have ever felt as though you or any member of your close units (whether at home, at work, or in your intimate relationships) have a crippling deficiency in EI, there is cause for concern, sure, but all is not lost. Unlike a person's intelligence and personality – which are both constant and inherent – a person's EI is, in large part, acquired and thus improvable. With enough determination and practice, your workplace, family, circles of friends, romantic partner will all soon enjoy the numerous benefits from enhancing your EI.

EI is believed to originate from where a person's "emotional brain" and "rational brain" intersect. The pathways for EI begin in the physical brain -- at the spinal cord. Your primary senses send its signals here and must travel to the front of your brain where the rationalizing of any experience occurs. But before these sensory signals reach this "thinking area", they first travel through your limbic system where emotions are spawned. This is why you experience an emotional reaction to events FIRST even before your rational mind is able to operate. EI, on the physiological realm, requires an unhindered communication between these rational and emotional centers of your brain.

Neurologists refer to the brain's ability to change as "plasticity". As you discover and practice new EI-related skills, the billions of neurons lined throughout the stretch between the rational and emotional centers of your brain branch off small "arms" (think of a growing tree) to make contact with the other cells. A single neuron can grow as much as 15,000 of these small "arms" to reach out to its neighbors. This chain reaction of growth facilitates the repetition of this new behavior in the future, under the right conditions.

In other words, as you "train your brain" by consistently practicing emotionally intelligent behaviors, your brain builds the pathways necessary to turn these behaviors into habits. It won't be long before you begin intelligently responding to your surroundings without needing to even think about it. And as your brain continuously reinforces these new behaviors, the neural connections that were the pathways of your former emotionally destructive behaviors will die off as your brain has learned to limit the use for these.

As earlier discussed, emotional intelligence begins with self-awareness. While some people may believe that they are not "emotional beings", closer inspection will reveal that we all live in an emotional state. Sometimes you are angry; sometimes you are sad; other times you are delighted. Each of us are always, always operating in an emotional state, on some level. This is where self-awareness becomes instrumental. Getting along and influencing people isn't about how smart you are or whether you have the highest educational achievement among everybody. Being an influential factor in the lives of people you live with has more to do with how you handle pressure and how well you connect to others by way of your behavior.

Help your discovery of self along by asking a leader, a friend, peer mentor, or your romantic partner to provide you with sincere and candid feedback about you. If it's at work and you are in a supervisory capacity, you could find out how much impact you have on people by eliciting feedback from them anonymously. Reach out to people who matter to you and spend quality time with them. Strive for all your interactions to help you gain a perspective as to how others perceive you. They key is to keep an open mind while listening to what others have to say. Do not get defensive when you receive less-than-glowing feedback. The first step toward a greater, more genuine self-awareness could be a tough one to take. But be assured that it will also be one of the most important and most rewarding steps you will ever take in your life.

And once you have a much clearer picture of who you are, the next logical step to take is to work at improving your EI and, in turn, your abilities for making sound decisions. The first task at hand in this glorious endeavor is to develop important skills that will help you control and manage overpowering stress and skills that will develop your abilities for effective communication.

You can begin building your EI by reducing stress, keeping your focus, and staying connected to yourself and others through these five important skills. These five important skills are divided into two categories: Managing Overwhelming Stress and Communicating Effectively. We will begin with an overview of these five key skills for improving your EI.

Managing Overwhelming Stress and the skills you need to learn:

Skill #1: Efficiently reduce stress in different situations. As nobody can truly predict all situations one will encounter down the line, getting your body "stress-ready" may be one of the most basic first steps you can take. You may avoid stimulants like alcohol, caffeine or nicotine, exercise regularly, sleep right, keep a journal, etc. There are numerous ways to keeping spry and immune to stress.

Skill #2: Acknowledge your emotions. Identifying your emotions and acknowledging its possible causes will deter you from becoming overwhelmed by them.

Communicating Effectively and the skills you need to learn:

Skill #3: Hone your nonverbal communication skills. Keeping your unspoken actions or reactions in check will only aid you in being misunderstood. Likewise, doing so helps you connect emotionally to others.

Skill #4: Rely on humor and play in the face of challenging situations. How many times have you been told to "lighten up!" in the face of stressful situations? Keeping your sense of humor can be an effective mechanism for dealing with stress. Jokes or witty conversation draws people closer to you. Also, finding humor in a stiuation helps you to view one situation in different ways.

Skill #5: Confidently resolve conflicts positively. Conflict is a natural part of any relationship. It is not reasonable (or realistic) to expect two individuals to always agree on everything. The key here is not to avoid or flee conflict, but to learn how to resolve it in a positive way. When handled in a positive and respectful manner, conflict can actually present an opportunity to strengthen the bond between two people.

How to Master those 5 EI-Improving Skills

The essential skills needed for improving EI can be learned by anyone, at any given time in one's life. The difference, though, lies in learning about how to improve your EI *and* actually applying what you have learned to your life.

Knowing what you should do is only half the battle; having the will to carry it out, especially when you're inundated with stress. As we all know, stress is a fierce enemy – it can come at you from all fronts and has the power to seize the best of intentions. Reading up and educating yourself about EI is simply not enough. It is imperative that you practice these EI-improving skills in your day to day life. When you've decided that you would truly want to begin learning how to improve your EI, the first important step is to fortify your behavior towards stress. You will need to exercise standing up to pressure and overcome stress as it comes at any moment.

Guage situations more accurately by keeping stress at bay

The first step to reducing stress is to recognize what it feels like to you. How does your body feel when you're under a lot of pressure? Do you have unexplained headaches? Are your muscles tight or sore? Are your brows furrowed? Your hands clenched? Is your breathing rapid or shallow? Be conscious of your physical responses to stress as this will help regulate tension when it comes.

As everyone reacts differently to stress, you will need to specifically identify your own ways of responding to stress. For example, if you notice that you become quick to anger or easily agitated under pressure, you will need to practice or engage in stress-relieving activities that calms you down. Deep breathing exercises are usually helpful in reigning in your nerves in the face of high pressure situations. It aids your body in counteracting against the physical effects of stress by slowing down your heart rate and lowering your blood pressure. Give yourself a quiet a 5-minute break where you can focus on your breathing. Sit up straight, close your eyes, and place a hand on your belly. Slowly inhale through your nose, feeling the breath enter your abdomen and visualize it as it work its way to the top of your head. Keep following the breath's track as it makes its way back to the abdomen as you exhale through your mouth. This 5-minute break also helps you avoid saying or doing things that you will likely regret later on.

On the other hand, if feeling depressed or withdrawing behavior is your typical stress response, what you will need are more stimulating stress-relieving activities. A 30-minute run on the treadmill or a dozen laps on the pool, maybe? You don't need to run in order to get what they call the "runner's high". If you are limited in a more confined vicinity, keep in mind that all forms of exercise can help calm anxiety and ease depression. Less strenuous exercise like yoga or walking aids the brain to release "feel-good" neurochemicals (like endorphins) and by giving your body a chance to practice how to cope with stress. You can go for a brisk walk around the block, take the stairs up and down a few flights, or get into stretching exercises such as head rolls or shoulder shrugs.

If you tend to "hang" (like an overworked computer that's running multiple applications at once) – speeding up in some tasks while slowing down on most others – you will definitely need stress-relieving activities that will offer you both comfort and stimulation. Something like a bowl of your favorite ice cream while watching a thought-provoking movie could do the trick. Better yet, reach out. Your social circle is one of your best bets for handling stress. Talk to your most trusted BFF or sound off on your basketball buddies -- ideally face to face, though hearing their voice over the phone works, too. Share what's going on. You can gain fresh perspective while keeping your social connections alive and strong.

One technique of reducing stress quickly is to engage one, some, or all of your physical senses. Yes, your sense of sight, sound, smell, taste, and/or touch. Each person is unique in how he or she responds to sensory stimulation, so you need to find things that are soothing and/or energizing to you. Let's say you're a visual person -- you can relieve stress by surrounding yourself with inspiring images or scenery. If you respond more to sound, a wind chime, your favourite song, or the sound of crickets might help to quickly diminish your stress levels. Combine stimulation as necessary.

Finally, one technique that has proven to work with plenty of people, regardless of the type of their stress response behavior, is to keep a Gratitude Journal. Start a gratitude journal that you will commit to keep, or better yet, a number of journals (one on your bedside, one in your purse, and one on your work desk) to help you keep track of all the positive things in your life. Being thankful for the blessings you have received and continue to receive crosses out the negative thoughts and worries that you may be harboring. Use these journals to reflect back on good experiences like an innocent child flashing you a smile as you were walking in the park, a day of sunshine, an unexpected friendly stranger, and, of course, your thriving health. Do not neglect to celebrate accomplishments like learning a new skill at work or being introduced to a new hobby. When you feel that stress is starting to creep up on you, spend a few moments looking through your thankful notes and help yourself remember what truly matters in your life.

Reduce your relationship stress through emotional awareness

Difficult life circumstances such as not having enough money for the bills, loved ones with failing health, figuring out who does what of the seemingly endless work of running a household, or the escalating power struggles at work can all conspire to induce stress in all your relationships. How the two people involved in the relationship talks over these stressful circumstances either alleviates or intensifies the already brewing-tension caused by the root problem (or problems). Marital, platonic, or parental arguments are the last thing you need when you're trying to deal with an already-tough situation.

Some situations in any relationship may trigger questions such as:

Will this relationship last?

Am I truly liked/loved/respected?

Is there equality here?

Am I secure here?

These questions are the typical sources of stress, especially in romantic relationships or marriage. Add to this hot-pot of touchy subjects the unfortunate inability of the people involved to communicate. More stress. Couples who lack healthy communication abilities can inadvertently antagonize each other more by provoking the five concerns above. Simultaneously, they worsen the stress in their relationship by being unable to come up with productive solutions to the problems they have or will encounter in the future.

When communicating with another person you are in a relationship with, resist the urge to start your sentences with *"you--"*. Susan Heitler, Ph.D.[24] refers to sentences like these as "crossovers". This is because when someone begins a sentence with *"you--"*, there is a semblance of "crossing over boundaries of the other person's space. These are easily construed as an "invasion" with the purpose to criticize, dictate, and an uncertain (therefore, possibly unfair) estimation of the other person's thoughts and feelings. Make it a point, instead, to use *"I--"* messages, accompanied by relevant questions. Talk only about *your* own thoughts and feelings or ask about your partner's. Do away with assuming or speaking for the other person. Ask.

As you try to gain a clearer perspective of your relationship partner's emotions, strive to stay connected with your emotions at all times in that you objectively identify how you truly feel. And then recognize (and admit) how these feelings are influencing your thoughts and, eventually, your actions. Doing this keeps you calm and grounded and so you will be able to focus better during high-tension situations and avoid further conflict with others in the relationship.

There are people who may come across as "emotionally disconnected". These people have likely had traumatizing negative childhood or recent experiences that have taught them to respond to stress by shutting off strong emotions like anger, sadness, joy, and fear. Have you noticed this kind of repressive behavior in yourself? Remind yourself that though you may try to deny, distort, or ignore your strongest feelings, you can never really remove them from your system. These will remain in you, unconscious of them as you may be. Without this kind of emotional awareness, you run the risk of becoming overwhelmed by your emotions in situations that may seem threatening. Worse, you will be held back from finally understanding your needs, what motivates you, and from communicating well with others.

If you wish to build up your self-awareness, begin by asking yourself these questions:

- Do you experience "flowing" feelings? Are you able to feel (and identify) one emotion after another as they occur, based on what you experience from moment to moment?
- Do your emotions come with physical sensations in, perhaps your stomach, chest, or legs?
- Do you experience subdued feelings and emotions, such as disapproval, sadness, fear, or delight – which are translated, even subtly, in your facial expressions or body language?
- Are you able to experience intense feelings that are strong enough to catch both your and others' attention?
- Do your emotions figure in how you make decisions?

If any of these experiences approach you as unfamiliar, it is likely that your emotions are muted or "turned off". For you to become more emotionally healthy and more emotionally intelligent, you must connect with your core emotions, acknowledge them, and genuinely accept them. Remember, emotional awareness can be achieved no matter where you are in your life. But if you haven't quite figured out how to manage the stress in your life, it's important to accomplish that first. When you are able to manage stress, you will be far more comfortable connecting with your strong or unpleasant emotions, changing the way you experience them, and appropriately responding to these emotions.

Improve Your Non-Verbal Communication Skills

A good communicator has nearly excellent verbal skills and the ability to manage stress. But that's not all. Being a good communicator is the ability to convey the entirety of his or her message through both verbal and non-verbal language. More often than not, what you say plays a secondary role to how you say it: your gestures, tone and volume of voice, facial expressions, eye contact, and other body languages will communicate more of what you really mean. For you to genuinely capture the attention of others and build a real trustworthy connection, you will need to be conscious and remain in control of your physical language. With this, you should also learn how to read and respond accurately to other people's non-verbal signals as they communicate with you.

It pays to always remember that communication is not just about speech. Messages do not cease with the silence of the speaker. In fact, it is in the silence that the real depth of the message can be construed. Be aware of the non-verbal cues that you are sending out to other people. This helps making sure that what you are conveying matches what you are truly feeling.

If you are insisting that you are "fine", and yet your knuckles are white from being clenched or you are looking away, your body language is more concisely giving you away. This does not make you a very trustworthy communicator now, does it? Keep in mind that your non-verbal messages are quite powerful in eliciting a sense of trust, excitement, interest, a desire for deeper connection in others. And so, these non-verbal signals of yours can be just as potent in prompting distrust, disinterest, confusion, or fear.

Effective non-verbal communication depends much on one's ability to respond well to stress, recognizing emotions, and understanding the cues that one conveys and receives. When you have a good handle on your emotions, then you will be able to react positively to stress. Thus, you will be able to consciously send off situation-appropriate body language and at the same time be objectively receptive of the non-verbal signals that others give out.

When you communicate, it is always important to focus on the other person. Stay away from misunderstandings or misinterpretation by keeping your mind present in all conversations as they happen. Daydreaming or thinking of something else unrelated mutes the words, non-verbal signals, and the meaning that the other person is conveying.

Eye contact is essential in every conversation. When you are able to consistently make direct eye contact when speaking or communicating with others, it conveys to the other party that you are interested in what they have to say. If you are giving a presentation at work, establish eye contact with as many members of the audience as possible. It tells them that you are confident about all the information that you are presenting. Making direct eye contact makes people more comfortable with you and assures them that you are credible enough for them to communicate with you in return. Eye contact indicates interest and will keep the conversation flowing. Keeping eye contact will allow you to pick up a lot of non-verbal messages, too. Furthermore, consistent eye contact keeps you alert in understanding another person's responses.

Also, the tone of your voice and the sound reactions you make are indications of your thoughts without you even needing to speak. For instance, if you receive instructions from a manager and you promptly grunt, you are showing your manager your candid disapproval and may imply an unwillingness to follow. Your tone or verbal sounds are likewise potent indications of your anger, frustration or distrust. Avoid highly audible and deliberately repetitive sighing or speaking in high-pitched tones. These make you very unprofessional and uncooperative. Speak softly and calmly. Assure the other person that you are in it for the good of everyone.

Monitor your posture. Slouching indicates that you are not interested in what a person is saying. Your body language during discussions is very important, whether at business meetings or family discussions. For example, swinging your leg back and forth while sitting in a meeting indicates to others you that you are bored, impatient, and utterly uninterested. Sit up straight, face, and turn your body towards others when speaking to them.

Pay attention, too, to your proximity to others. Encroaching on other people's personal space affects how they react to you. Different cultures regard proximity in unique ways, so take notice if the person you are communicating with is uncomfortable. This could mean that you are standing too close for comfort and should provide a respectful distance between the two of you. The amount of physical space given can convey certain emotions, like a person who is behaving aggressively is likely standing too close to the other person, thus eliciting feelings of defensiveness, distrust, or dislike.

Rely on humor and play in the face of challenging situations

Play, humor, and laughter are life's natural remedies to stress. Keeping things relaxed and humorous will help you feel unburdened and allow for things to stay in perspective. Laughter reduces stress by keeping one's mood level and elevated, thus keeping one's nervous system stable and away from erratic behavior.

Playful communication can expand your EI and will certainly help you take difficulties in stride. As humor allows you to view a situation from a variety of perspectives, you can deal with your disappointments or frustrations more effortlessly. Appropriate and gentle humor will often be helpful in saying things that could otherwise be intensely offensive and the positive flow of communication can be invigorating for yourself, as well. You are then a better conversationalist in a positive exchange and you become quite creative in what you say and more open to seeing everything in new ways.

By all means, tell funny stories relevant to the difficulty at hand. Jokes are great, too, but others will likely find stories of something that actually happened to you to be a little more humorous, aside from side-stepping the possibility of offending others. Think of a few funny things that have happened to you and tell those stories when appropriate. Keep your stories or jokes concise or direct to the point. In general, people have short attention spans, even moreso for light digressions off the actual topic. Keep your story quick, to the point, and tasteful.

The tricky part about this is, of course, avoiding jokes or humorous plays at situations that are "in bad taste". You need to be keenly aware of the people that make up your "audience" and what each may or may not find offensive to their sensibilities. This is why your best bet is self-deprecating humor, which we've learned to be a hallmark of self-awareness – the first element of EI. Self-deprecating humor, or putting yourself down for laughs, reduces the risk of offending others, however too much of it is not pleasant, too. Some people tend to overuse self-deprecating humor to fish for compliments. Other times, too much self-deprecating humor might be an indication of a suffering self-esteem.

Researchers from the Mind, Brain and Behaviour Research Centre (CIMCYC) have found that individuals who frequently resort to self-deprecating humor for the purpose of gaining others' approval through mocking of the self exhibit higher levels of psychological well-being.[25]

Harness your abilities of humorous or playful communication by actually allotting quality time for yourself to engage in recreation. Allowing yourself to regularly experience enjoyable activities helps you "loosen up". Join a sports club where you can indulge in your favorite sport; find a group who regularly meets to play board games; take time to stop and play with babies and pets; or perhaps work on your garden everyday. Surround yourself with like-minded individuals who appreciate playful banter as much as possible.

Confidently resolve conflicts positively

Conflict and disagreements are a natural and inevitable part of any relationship. It is hardly possible for two different people to have exactly the same needs, opinions, and expectations. Uniqueness in people is nature's best way to encourage learning, after all. Resolving conflict in a healthy and constructive manner strengthens trust between people. When conflict doesn't come with the trappings of threat or punishment, it promotes creativity, individuality, and security in relationships.

Mastery of the four earlier skills (reducing stress, acknowledging emotions, non-verbal communication, and play) contributes substantially to your ability to manage conflict in your relationships. As soon as you have learned how to effectively manage the stress in your life, how to remain emotionally "there", how to communicate well non-verbally, and how to rely on humor in appropriate situations, you will easily be able to ease misunderstanding before they take any turn for the worse.

It pays to be reminded that Issues don't come up because there's a conflict. They come up because the difference in views is not addressed in a constructive or productive way. When conflict is allowed to fester, it can make everyone involved turn into unproductive individuals and the work environment starts to feel "poisoned" or tainted.

The crux of the matter of conflicts is that a lot of people don't bother to even learn how to handle conflict at all. It is quite tempting to instead spend most of our time and energy trying to avoid it. Begin learning about effective conflict resolution by changing the way you actually view conflict. All our lives, we have likely been taught to believe that conflict is, plain and simply, bad. Since a person's mindset determines how he or she approaches a situation and heavily influences his or her actions, endeavor now to start regarding conflict as an opportunity actually to actually fix a problem. This way, disagreements will no longer anger you as much and you can be more objective in determining productive solutions to whatever difficulty people are arguing over.

One of the biggest misconceptions that people typically have when it comes to arguments is thinking that they have to "win." Their primary purpose for getting into arguments is to convince the other person that they are right and this other person is wrong. Instead, be more positive and consider that it is likely that the reason this other person is disagreeing with you is because they are seeing things that are not visible to you. The blind insistence on always being right is a sure-fire way to damage any relationship and deter any team effort, especially in cases of work disputes. Make it a point to take the time to listen to the other person or group. Try to understand where they are coming from. Ask solid questions that will help you understand (and possibly appreciate) the other person's position. And once you have a clearer picture of the other person's position, understand why they are so steadfast in holding on to it. Knowing what they believe in and why they believe in it will help you address their concerns more precisely, rather than just guessing. Doing it this way likewise helps you brainstorm together on better solutions.

It helps to strive to stay focused in the *Now*. Let go of past hurts and resentment so you can easily recognize the reality of a current circumstance. *Now* situations can present numerous opportunities for resolving *Past* hurts over conflicts. All you need is the positive attitude to help you discern these opportunities. Help yourself achieve this by learning to forgive other people for the hurt they might have caused you by their actions in the past. Resist the temptation to seek revenge or impose punishment. These are highly negative emotions that will have the tendency to drain you out.

When you have acquired the natural positivity in you that allows you to let go of the negative feeling from the past, you can move forward a lot smoothly by learning to "pick your battles". Choose the arguments you will get drawn into. Use your better judgment in deciding what is truly worth your time and energy to argue about and what is not.

The reality is that, in most conflicts, you are not going to end up with everything you expect or want. If you are attempting to resolve a conflict in a way that is most beneficial to your organization or unit, you will need to learn to choose your "battles" wisely. There is no need to argue over every single point. Figure out what areas are the most critical, then focus your brain power on those areas. As people say, do not "sweat the small stuff". Feeling the need to win on every single point of contention leaves many people missing out on opportunities to resolve a conflict.

The basic rule of thumb that you can adhere to when engaged in a charged argument or a disagreement in views, is that what matters in all discussions, whether at work or with your more personal relationships, is coming away from it with the feeling that one had been treated justly, believing that what they had to say had been "heard", regardless of the outcome or resolution achieved. The keyword here is "collaboration."

Yes, it is always important to address the points of disagreement. But it is likewise necessary to focus on the areas of agreement when trying to resolve a conflict. Aim to discover the common ground. Tap on the spirit of teamwork by finding the areas of commonality. Always remind yourselves that you are trying to achieve a common goal. This gives both of you a deeper sense of purpose and belonging and gives you both something to build on. Again, resolving conflict is not about winning the argument. It's more about working together to uncover the most effective solution to whatever challenges you are facing. Resolve to handle the conflict in a collaborative nature. This is one of the best, most efficient ways to turn conflict into something that is most beneficial to the overall objective.

A key component in resolving conflict is keeping your "eyes on the prize". In the face of working out a conflict, it can be quite easy to lose sight of what you are actually trying to achieve. When you feel that the actual purpose is getting lost in the more trivial points of the conflict, you should always steer the conversation back onto the track of what you and the other person are originally trying to accomplish collectively. Remember, conflict is a critical and inevitable element in achieving your team's goals, and so conflict should always be regarded as a tool – not an obstacle.

It takes two people to sustain an argument for as long as they allow it to last. Even if you still disagree with another person's views or opinions, you can always choose to disengage from the conflict. People with high EI know how to "agree to disagree". The high road is always open and the choice is always yours to take.

It is not always possible for everyone to contract a professional psychotherapist. Did you know that Freud actually "analyzed" himself?[26] The journey to better EI all begins with learning how to listen to your own feelings. It may not always be easy, but training yourself to stay attuned to your emotions and studying how you react to each is a significant step in improving your EI that you can not do without.

In the book *Self-Analysis* (1945), the author Karen Horney shares the belief that people can "treat" the self with or without the aid of a therapist.[27] Progress is made and monitored between sessions, whenever the person manifests a genuine readiness. In Self-Analysis[28], Horney explained that many people endure the psychological effects that result from abiding to false ideas that manifest as "neurotic trends". Horney reiterates that each person must veer away from these false ideas and, instead, look inward to the self for true beliefs and that self-analysis is a useful tool in discovering the truth about the self, in most cases. According to Horney, there are a number of neurotic trends that should be identified, understood, and ideally "deleted" from one's system of beliefs. Horney claims that a person can observe his or her own behavior and make positive changes as he or she sees necessary. Life will become significantly better, once these neurotic trends have been removed.

Horney lists ten types of neurotic trends in her book. These include a person's need for:

1) affection

2) a partner

3) restricting the scope of life

4) power (the control and power of will)

5) exploiting others

6) prestige

7) admiration

8) personal achievement and ambition

9) self-sufficiency

10) perfection and superiority

These needs in a person are termed 'neurotic' because, according to Horney, they do not fully represent human values or what a person might really want. Neurotic trends interfere with most, if not all, facets of life, and anything that has a semblance of fulfilling such allow the person to mistakenly believe that "all is well".

First understanding the individual's motives is essential if any change in the individual's behavior is sought – this summarizes Horney's form of psychotherapy. If a person's motives are contradictory of his or her neurotic trends, this likely causes a suffering in the person as the person ends up struggling to overcome these resistances. In self-analysis, the use of free association is recommended, instead of straightforward intellectual thinking. Free association is the mental process where one word or image may spontaneously suggest an entirely unrelated idea or image and can promote understanding of one's neurotic trends. The person should write down his or her reactions to each free association imagery, and these responses are used as a tool for psychologically clarifying and overcoming the resistances. However, the person who does not have any background on or knowledge about psychoanalysis will unlikely gain any benefits from free association exercises, Horney says. Therefore, the author recommends for anyone who is endeavoring to conduct self-analysis to still contract a professional therapist occasionally.

According to Horney, the goal in Freud's psychoanalysis can be summarized by the brief phrase: "to gain freedom from" (1945, p. 21). Horney furthers this outlook in her own psychoanalysis as: "by rendering a person free from inner bondages, make him free for the development of his best potentialities" (pp. 21- 22). Goals for the person seeking changes in behavior should always be positive, with appropriate incentives that will motivate him or her to grow and achieve his or her full potential.

You have the capacity to observe yourself better than anyone else. You have a unique vantage point, by default. A therapist schedules you for, what? One or two hours in a week, while you can observe yourself constantly. A trained therapist uses different psychological techniques during treatment, but you will have much more time to monitor your own thoughts and behavior. This is why the use of self-analysis is most compelling. You do not require training to observe yourself. You know perfectly how and what you think, say, or do. All you need is a commitment to be honest to yourself at all times and not allow your emotions to become blind to unconscious forces (1945, p. 27). If you wish to understand the reasons behind your difficulties, you must start identifying your own neurotic trends and other motivations that contradict them.

Simply put, what you practice is what you become good at. Self-analysis is only a matter of constant monitoring of the self; of self-awareness; of knowing how you contribute to the community you belong in and knowing how you are perceived by your immediate environment. Self analysis is illuminating and quite instrumental in developing an individual's personality. Think of it this way: as humans, we all make mistakes, but learning from these mistakes is what makes the real difference. For example, if you get annoyed with your spouse, roommate, or friend for not cooking the dish that you requested, you best can analyze the real reason behind the frustration. Did you get annoyed because you did not get the dish you wanted? What does that imply? You might realize that you were thinking only about yourself and was quite ungrateful for the dish that was actually prepared for you with time and effort. In this analogy, if you truly have the desire for self-improvement, the next time your spouse, roommate, or friend does not cook the food of your choice, you will instead be grateful for what was actually cooked for you.

Once you have a firmer grasp of your own emotions and subsequent responses, it will become easy to stay in touch with other people's emotions, eventually. Make it a habit to never interrupt or attempt to change the subject whenever the emotional temperature starts to feel uncomfortable. Distracting ourselves and others throughout the course of a communication will only direct your relationship to negative turns. Instead, perhaps take a breather and ask yourself "how am I feeling?" And if you are able to answer this objectively, it is likely that you can also find out what's really causing this emotional response in you. This exercise allows you to pick up on communication in a more level-headed and rational manner.

Try not to judge or "edit" your feelings in haste. Never try to set your feelings aside before allowing yourself the chance to think them through. *"What just happened?" "What is causing this emotion in me?" "How would I like to act after feeling this way?"* These are the questions you need to always ask yourself, especially in the face of intense emotions. Remember that emotions ebb and flow naturally. Do not cut off the "wave" before it gets the chance to tide up to its peak. When you try to suppress a certain emotion before it has reached its natural levels, there is a chance that you respond inappropriately and/or prematurely to the emotion – something that you might come to regret later on. Always remember that the important thing is you are able to stay focused and rational as you ride out the rise and fall of your emotions.

Another healthy exercise for improved EI is to try to see if there is any pattern to your feelings. Try and see if you can find a connection between this instance of a particular emotion and other instances when this same emotion occurred. Whenever an intense or a challenging emotion arises, stop and ask yourself, *"When have I felt this same feeling in the past?"* Look for similarities in surrounding events, people, settings, etc. Doing so may be helpful to you in realizing whether this current emotional state is elicited by your current situation, or if this is actually stemming from a past experience. Emotional reactions drawn from a past event in your own life may be harmful to those who you are in a relationship with at present. Keep in mind that this other person may not have been around yet then to have witnessed where this emotion is coming from. And so, purging residual emotion upon him or her now may just be, simply put, unjust.

Connect your thoughts and feelings. Whenever you feel that something is odd or out of place, it always pays to pause and ask yourself what you actually think about that oddity. It may happen that an emotion will contradict other governing emotional states, and that's okay. It is normal to feel a certain way about something when you generally are feeling the opposite. Think of it this way: listening to your feelings is quite like a judge or jury listening to all testimonies in a court case before coming to a decision. Only by acknowledging and admitting all the evidence can you justly arrive at a final "verdict".

Tune in to your physical reactions. A "knot" in your gut as you make your way to work could be an indication that your job is actually a source of stress for you. A flutter in your chest every time you catch a glimpse of the new guy in the Accounting department could be your cue to ask him out. Paying attention to these physical reactions in you and the possible underlying emotions gives you the opportunity to process emotions with reason.

After all these self-awareness exercises and you still can't seem to fully understand your real feelings, by all means go ask someone else. We could all use "fresh eyes" to see the bigger picture more clearly, sometimes. Seek out someone you trust and who knows you well and ask for their help in judging how you might be feeling. Accept their observations and feedback about how you are acting or how you are generally coming across to other people. Often enough, an outsider's point of view will surprise you... and illuminate you.

Find a way to your unconscious feelings and keep an open channel. A person's unconscious is where a large part of the mind's functions happen; it is the receptacle for instinctive skills, the source of kept (and often repressed) memories of one's more traumatic experiences, intuition, and dreams; and where a person processes information. Unconscious feelings, then, are those that are not readily visible on a person's "surfaces". These emotions are invisible to others and to the actual person himself.

If you wish to connect with your unconscious feelings, you may try free association. This exercise is done by going into a relaxed state and then allowing your thoughts to wander unhindered so you can watch where they lead. Also, try to seek the closest credible interpretation of your dreams. Make it a point to keep a journal on your bedside so you can write down the vivid parts of your dream to the best of your recollection first thing when you wake up from it. Pay extra attention to dreams that recur or dreams that provoke extreme emotions.

And while we are on the subject of keeping journals –
writing your thoughts and feelings down on paper is a
very fruitful exercise. Research has shown that putting
pen to paper with your thoughts and emotions help
profoundly in staying connected with yourself. The self-
awareness that can be derived when you read back
your thoughts and feelings is immeasurable. This
exercise surely speeds things along in terms of a better
knowing of yourself.

Everyday, set aside quiet time for yourself when you
can have an inward conversation and ask, *"How do I
feel today?"* Evaluate your sense of well-being by rating
it on a scale of 0 to 100. Log your scores daily in a
journal. Periodically (like at the end of each week or
month) review your entries, taking special note of days
when your emotions might've felt extreme (those
emotions that you've rated close to 90 and above).
Take the time to reflect on any associations or
connections between those days. You might notice a

pattern of behavior or similar experiences that are triggers for such high emotions.

And when you feel that you have journeyed inward at such depth and substance, it might be time to start shifting your focus outward. This is especially true if what you have discovered in your journey towards self-awareness are more negative than positive, it might be a good time to take a break. Consider looking outside for help – professional guidance, if need be. There could be some emotions triggered by insurmountable trauma from the past that might entail a more systematic process to rehabilitate. The key is to acknowledge the emotion and seek help as necessary. Merely accepting a harmful emotion as just and leaving it unanswered might cause it to escalate into more overwhelming emotions that could be triggered by unforeseen factors down the road.

At the end of the day, emotional intelligence is not all about the ability to look within you, but also about being able to make, preserve, and strengthen your connections with everyone around you.

Conclusion

We all have understood at this point that emotional intelligence is the very powerful ability to manage our own emotions, as well as others'. We have appreciated how this ability can only impact all of our relationships positively. May none of us ever neglect to sustain the mind and body with healthy habits. Emotionally intelligent habits affect how we perceive situations, how situations evoke thoughts, and ultimately, how our thoughts contribute to how we feel and express our reactions.

Taking proactive steps in keeping your emotions under control will only help you in the best ways in all aspects of your life. This elusive ability of regulating one's feelings will allow you to manage your emotions in stressful conditions and develop your instincts, instead of always succumbing to the aggravatingly typical fight, flight, or freeze responses. If you take the brave steps down this beaten path of building your EI, you are assured of nothing but intelligent, balanced, and well-informed decisions throughout your life.

I cannot reiterate it enough, how important a highly developed EI is to one's career growth. We've now learned that a majority of hiring businesses actually utilize EI-based assessment instruments in recruitment and in evaluating existing manpower for potential for success.

If you are eyeing more responsibilities or a promotion to an actual leadership role (which comes with more responsibilities, by default) at work, your EI levels will likely be a key determinant. EI is essential for leadership responsibilities as higher positions typically translate more people reporting to you.

Or you could be at a point in your life when you are starting to yearn for *that* relationship that will see you to the twilight of your life or just more meaningful relationships, in general. You've also possibly suspected at least once that you could use some help with how you behave under pressure. You might have made a string of decisions you regret 'till now. Whatever crossroad you are at right now, what matters most is that you *are* at a turning point. Moments in a person's life when he or she decides to undertake a definitive change is always good. Though you will not always be able to predict all outcomes, change is, at the very least, the right step into *a* direction.

References

1.   Mayer, J.D., Geher, G. (1996) 'Emotional intelligence and the identification of emotion', Elsevier, 22 (2) [online]. Available at https://www.sciencedirect.com/science/article/pii/S01602896 96900112 (Accessed 26 November 2918)

2.   Ohrnberger, J. (2017) 'The relationship between physical and mental health: a mediation analysis', Elsevier, 195 [online]. Available at https://www.sciencedirect.com/science/article/pii/S02779536 17306639 (Accessed 26 November 2018)

3.   Salovey, P. and Mayer, J. D. (1990) 'Emotional Intelligence', Imagination, Cognition and Personality, 9(3), pp. 185–211. doi: 10.2190/DUGG-P24E-52WK-6CDG.

4.   Joseph D. L., Newman D. A. (2010). Emotional intelligence: an integrative meta-analysis and cascading model. J. Appl. Psychol. 95, 54–78. 10.1037/a0017286 [PubMed] [CrossRef]

5.   Mayer J. D., Salovey P., Caruso D. (2002). Mayer-Salovey-Caruso Emotional Intelligence Test (MSCEIT) User's Manual Test. Toronto, ON: Multi-Health Systems.

6.   Salovey P., Mayer J. D., Goldman S. L., Turvey C., Palfai T. P. (1995). "Emotional attention, clarity, and repair: exploring emotional intelligence using the trait meta-mood scale," in Emotion, Disclosure, and Health, ed. Pennebaker J. W., editor. (Washington, DC: American Psychological Association;), 125–154.

7.   Bar-On R. (2004). "The bar-on emotional quotient inventory (EQ-i): rationale, description and summary of psychometric properties," in Measuring Emotional Intelligence: Common Ground and Controversy, ed. Geher G., editor. (Hauppauge, NY: Nova Science Publishers), 115–145.

8.   Schutte N. S., Malouff J. M., Thorsteinsson E. B., Bhullar N., Rooke S. E. (2007). A meta-analytic investigation of the relationship between emotional intelligence and health. Pers. Individ. Dif. 42, 921–933. 10.1016/j.paid.2006.09.003 [CrossRef]

9.   Martins A., Ramalho N., Morin E. (2010). A comprehensive meta-analysis of the relationship between Emotional Intelligence and health. Pers. Individ. Dif. 49, 554–564. 10.1016/j.paid.2010.05.029 [CrossRef]

10.   Zeidner M., Matthews G., Roberts R. D. (2012). The emotional intelligence, health and well-being nexus: what have we learned and what have we missed? Appl. Psychol.

Health Well Being 4, 1–30. 10.1111/j.1758-0854.2011.01062.x [PubMed] [CrossRef]

11.   Cabello R., Fernández-Berrocal P. (2015b). Under which conditions can introverts achieve happiness? Mediation and moderation effects of the quality of social relationships and emotion regulation ability on happiness. PeerJ 3:e1300. 10.7717/peerj.1300 [PMC free article] [PubMed][CrossRef]

12.   Sánchez-Álvarez N., Extremera N., Fernández-Berrocal P. (2015). The relation between emotional intelligence and subjective well-being: a meta-analytic investigation. J. Posit. Psychol. 11, 276–285. 10.1080/17439760.2015.1058968 [CrossRef]

13.   Côté S. (2014). Emotional intelligence in organizations. Annu. Rev. Organ. Psychol. Organ. Behav.1, 459–488. 10.1146/annurev-orgpsych-031413-091233 [CrossRef]

14.   Mavroveli S., Petrides K. V., Sangareau Y., Furnham A. (2009). Exploring the relationships between trait emotional intelligence and objective socio-emotional outcomes in childhood. Br. J. Educ. Psychol. 79, 259–272. 10.1348/000709908X368848 [PubMed] [CrossRef]

15.   García-Sancho E., Salguero J. M., Fernández-Berrocal P. (2014). Relationship between emotional

intelligence and aggression: a systematic review. Aggress. Violent Behav. 19, 584–591. 10.1016/j.avb.2014.07.007 [CrossRef]

16.   Kun B., Demetrovics Z. (2010). Emotional intelligence and addictions: a systematic review. Subst. Use Misuse 45, 1131–1160. 10.3109/10826080903567855 [PubMed] [CrossRef]

17.   Gutiérrez-Cobo MJ, Cabello R, Fernández-Berrocal P. The Three Models of Emotional Intelligence and Performance in a Hot and Cool go/no-go Task in Undergraduate Students. Front Behav Neurosci. 2017;11:33. Published 2017 Feb 22. doi:10.3389/fnbeh.2017.00033

18.   TalentSmart 'About emotional intelligence', TalentSmart [online]. Available at http://www.talentsmart.com/about/emotional-intelligence.php (Accessed 3 December 2018)

19.   Grasz, J. (2011) 'Seventy-one percent of employers say they value emotional intelligence over IQ, according to CareerBuilder survey', CareerBuilder [online]. Available at https://www.careerbuilder.ca/share/aboutus/pressreleasesde tail.aspx?id=pr652&sd=8%2f18%2f2011&ed=8%2f18%2f209 9 (Accessed 3 December 2018)

20.   Mayer, J.D. (2009) 'What emotional intelligence is and is not', Psychology Today [online]. Available at

https://www.psychologytoday.com/intl/blog/the-personality-analyst/200909/what-emotional-intelligence-is-and-is-not (Accessed 2 December 2018)

21.   Crow, S. (2018) '30 ways that emotional intelligence can make you better at everything', Best Life [online]. Available at https://bestlifeonline.com/emotional-intelligence-improves-relationships/ (Accessed 2 December 2018)

22.   Dfarhud, D., Malimir, M., Khanahmadi, M.(2014) 'Happiness and health: the biological factors – systematic review article', Iranian Journal of Public Health [online] 43 (11). Available at https://www.ncbi.nlm.nih.gov/pmc/articles/PMC4449495/ (Accessed 5 December 2018)

23.   TalentSmart '9 habits of highly emotionally intelligent people', TalentSmart [online]. Available at http://www.talentsmart.com/articles/9-Habits-of-Highly-Emotionally-Intelligent-People-2147446657-p-1.html (Accessed 5 December 2018)

24.   Heitler, S. (2013) 'Stress in relationships: 10 sources and their antidotes', Psychology Today [online]. Available at https://www.psychologytoday.com/us/blog/resolution-not-conflict/201305/stress-in-relationships-10-sources-and-their-antidotes (Accessed 12 December 2018)

25.   University of Granada (2018) 'Self-deprecating humor promotes psychological well-being, study reveals' Medical Xpress [online]. Available at https://medicalxpress.com/news/2018-02-self-deprecating-humour-psychological-well-being-reveals.html (Accessed 12 December 2018)

26.   Chiriac, J. 'Sigmund Freud's self-analysis', Sigmund Freud – Biography [online]. Available at http://www.freudfile.org/self_analysis.html (Accessed 11 December 2018)

27.   Waxman, R. 'Review of self-analysis (Horney, 1945)', The Love of Wisdom [online]. Available at http://www.robertwaxman.com/id94.html (Accessed 12 December 2018)

28.   Horney, K. 1945, Self-analysis, W. W. Norton & Company, Inc., London.

The Enneagram Of Personality

Why Discovering Your Unique Personality Type Is Essential For Your Personal Growth

By

Arthur Canfield

Preface

The subject of Psychology is truly an interesting field of study. It goes into the human mind and how it actually works. This field gives us a bird's eye view of what can actually go on inside a human being's head when he reacts a certain way or says something that may not be considered as a common response to a situation.

These idiosyncrasies are what make humans unique when compared to other species. It is what makes us stand out among other life forms here on earth. And so, this book aims to explore the many facets of the human mind and how it ought to function in society.

This book was written solely to become a beacon of knowledge regarding personality and what it means to be human in the truest sense of the word. Out of the curious mind of the author, himself came about his quest for knowledge regarding wanting to understand and comprehend the inner workings of human personality as a whole.

The author also wants to understand a human's basic need to connect with others of the same kind. What are the building blocks of interpersonal connection as it relates to human personality?

By reading this book, we hope that we can help you understand the inner workings of the personality of man so as to help you interact with your fellow human better down the road.

It is also our hope to help each reader discover why they came to be the way they are through the study of the different interrelated personality types that make up the human being. How do these personality types relate to one another within the same and different individuals?

In the subsequent paragraphs, we will try to help individuals realize their unique potential. What can they bring to the table in terms of their skill, talent, and innate gifts?

If you want to learn more about the Enneagram of Personality, who you are as an individual and what you can actually do to function better as a productive citizen both in business and in your personal life, please do not hesitate to read on.

You will surely not regret doing so. You might even end up becoming a better friend, relative and member of the community because of this.

Introduction

The human being is truly a complex scientific enigma that is surely interesting to study. We are intelligent and dynamic organisms that are able to compose clear thought and concepts all on our own.

We are known to be independent and unique in terms of behavior and interaction; a true product of the natural evolution that has occurred and is still occurring all throughout the centuries.

However, inquisitive minds may ask why were we created as such? Why are we able to think for ourselves and formulate constructs that tend to change the course of our existence on this earth? These are just two of the questions that this book aims to answer.

By the end of the book, we aim to achieve a few simple objectives as follows:

- Help the reader understand the basic definition and concepts surrounding the Enneagram of Human Personality and its continuous development.

- Provide scientific and medical explanations regarding concepts relating to the connections between the different personality types relating to the previous concept and the psychology behind this.

- Introduce some of the well-known figures that helped propel the discovery and further study of the Enneagram of Personality into the forefront of the psychological field.

- Give the reader a glimpse of what lies ahead in terms of related studies on the variously related personality types and its development as connected to societal innovation.

What Can You Expect?

In this particular book, we will discuss the Enneagram of Personality and what it actually means. It aims to answer the following questions:

- What are the different personality types?

- How to properly interact with each personality type?

- What are the thought processes of each personality type?

- Who are some of the most popular personalities/people that correspond to each number of the Enneagram?

- What are the positive and negative aspects of the nine personality types?

- What are the growth practices that could help improve each personality?

- How do you find out your specific personality type? Are there tools you can use?

- What do you do once you find out your specific personality type?

Additional Goals

It is our hope that after reading this particular book, you will be able to understand more about your own personality and how to deal with the interrelated, but different personality constructs within various individuals both directly and indirectly in the future.

We will also provide you with some tips regarding the different ways of dealing with the distinct personality types within the parameters of the Enneagram and in various situations contingent upon your own personal constructs of behavior.

This book will also discuss the basic figure relating to the Enneagram Figure of Personality. We will break down the nine different personality types relating to this figure and the basic motivations that build the framework of each individual personality type.

Through the different sections of the book, we will discuss both the positive and the negative aspects of personality and what you can do to modify your own personality if and when necessary.

After this, we will then give you an idea as to how each of these personality constructs, motivations and forms of behavior relate to one another to form the Enneagram of Personality. It will be an interesting discussion for sure.

Before we go any further, it is good to know that while the human personality is a vast and complicated subject to tackle, through this book, you will be able to understand what the term personality truly means and how it can affect your own individual view of your human existence.

You will further understand your own individual identity through the nine different types of personalities and what you can contribute to the world at large.

Interested to learn more? Continue to the next section.

Chapter One: The Basics of the Enneagram of Personality

Subchapter One: Understanding the 9 Various Enneagram Personality Types

There are many factors that contribute to human evolution. Some of these include the following:

- Physical Growth and Development
- Environment
- Human Interaction
- Nature
- Experiences

All these factors affect who we are as people. It helps shape our ideas and determine our initial belief system. These factors along with many others also shape our unique personality which can continue to evolve and change all throughout our lives as normal organisms.

This chapter will give us an idea as to the main definition of personality enneagram and how it is usually formed. In addition, we will also learn about some of the basic personality types as it relates to the Enneagram of Personality.

We will focus on learning about the different factors that affect the different personality types and how these factors determine human individuality in terms of the choices that are made and definitive decisions in life.

The readers will also be introduced to the basic proponents of this particular school of psychology. If you want to learn more about the Enneagram and what it entails, please do not hesitate to read. It is our hope that you learn more about yourself and others through this chapter and the preceding ones as well.

It is also our hope that this book may be able to provide pertinent information about the psychology of personality and how it can work to push for the human advantage and improvement down the line. So what are you waiting for? Go to the next section so that you may be able to find out more about the Enneagram Personality Paradigm and the different personality types that it houses.

Ascent and Descent

In science, the term ascent refers to the act of going up or advancing to a much higher plane of existence. Descent, on the other hand, refers to the exact opposite. It is a phenomenon wherein a person goes downward or degrades his or her level of existence depending on the situation itself.

In terms of the Enneagram of Personality, the terms ascent and descent take on slightly different meanings. According to this particular paradigm of the personality, you can view these terms as part of the evolutionary process of human beings and their personalities.

It means that depending on certain phases in their lives, the human personality changes and evolves into a much higher level of knowledge and perception. This has to do mainly with the types of interactions that they encounter, the thought processes and the human body and mind becoming transcendent at the end of each process.

It just basically refers to how the Enneagram of personality propels the individual to change his behavior according to the events that transpire within his own life cycle. He can have both heightened and lowered emotional responses to certain situations in his life especially traumatic events according to this psychological concept. It is therefore important for people with known Enneagram personality types to have proper support systems in order to successfully navigate through life.

Here are some of the most important people that can provide support for each personality type:

- Family

- Friends

- Significant others

- Co-workers

This support system may vary depending on the kind and quality of interpersonal relationships that each personality type has in their lives. Whatever kind of relationship each type may have, the important thing is that he is able to forge strong bonds with others.

As the saying goes, no man is an island and in order to become a healthy human being, one must have strong and steady connections to the outside world on a regular basis.

Meditation and Its Significance to Overall Personality Development

As mentioned earlier, ascent and descent are integral parts of the process of evolution within the personality Enneagram.

Meditation helps individuals to achieve this by ensuring that the physical body is able to transcend needs and wants so as to elevate itself into a much more knowledgeable plane of existence.

If this happens, the individual will be able to interact with other personalities in a much more calm and learned fashion. This has to do with the spiritual maturity and strength of the individual.

If you are able to transcend your personal biases, wants and needs, then you will be able to ascend to a much more peaceful way of thinking which can pave the way for you to help others more fully and to find your own calling in the near future.

There are many different personality types which correspond to different callings in life. These different personality types and callings will be discussed further in the next chapter of the book.

Meanwhile, as part of your meditation exercises, it is important that you are aware of how you breathe. Taking in and expelling oxygen from your body effectively will provide more focus and energy whenever you choose to meditate.

Did you know that there are nine different types of breathing practices that one should definitely take note of if they want to experience a much healthier condition during their journey in discovering their own personality type?

The mentioned breathing practices and how it affects the nine specific personality types physically, emotionally and spiritually will be discussed in the next chapters as well. We will also discuss the main advantages of these practices in terms of personality improvements and more positive effects on the personal interactions of these individuals.

Advantages of Breathing Exercises

If you undergo breathing exercises regularly, there are certain advantages that you can reap from these for your health, growth, and awareness. Here are some advantages as follows:

Deep breaths can help you experience both the physicality of the activity as well as the emotions that come with it.

It will help you relax even more and relieve you of distress and stress that tend to bog you down during the day.

Breathing has a calming effect on the body. It relieves the nervous system of unnecessary tension that can cause the body to freeze up whenever a stressful event happens.

Breathing can help us look inside ourselves even better. It can also provide us with clear thoughts so as to not have tension affect our own personal boundaries in the outside world.

Through this activity, we also become aware of our bodily functions and what kind of effect the external world has on it.

Deep breathing promotes self-awareness as part of personal development. If you are aware of your breath, it would be easy for you to pay attention to some of the little things that usually escape the human eye. Deep breathing can also help you become sharper and much more intelligent in your decision-making and interactions.

This is you should do it more often.

Various Known Practices

The Receptive Breathing Technique

In this particular process, you simply follow the breaths during meditation without having to change the pattern at all. The practitioner must pay attention to the physical sensations that you feel whenever you inhale and exhale. This way, you will become aware of your internal functions and see how well you are doing physically and mentally.

Active

This particular process gives us more energy when necessary. It can also help us reserve our strength whenever it is required. This particular type of breathing technique will make you aware of the different patterns involved when it comes to the nine various personality types of the Enneagram.

This type of breathing aims to sharpen your mind so that you would become more aware of your surroundings. It works in such a way that you take in air to gather if more energy from nature rather than to calm yourself down.

Now that you know the different kinds of techniques involved in natural breathing exercises, we will now move on to finding out the specific breathing patterns that are exclusive to the nine personality types in the Enneagram.

These nine breathing patterns will help one discover his own personality in a much more profound sense and a deeper level than before. Through some of these breathing exercises, the individual will be more aware of what makes him who he is as a unique individual apart from other people that might have similar personality traits.

If you would like to learn more, please do not hesitate to continue. The breathing patterns along with other pertinent information about personality will be discussed as part of the subsequent sections of the book.

Subchapter 2: The Enneagram Personality Paradigm: A View of the Different Personality Types

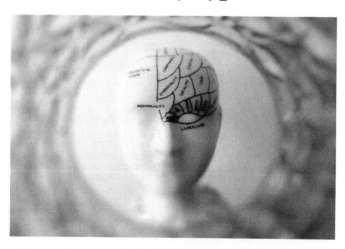

This section deals with understanding the different types and facets of human personality as related to the Enneagram Personality Paradigm.

This being said, we cannot hope to fathom the different types of personalities unless we make an effort to know what the word truly means first.

What is Personality?

According to the Merriam-Webster Dictionary, the term personality can be defined as the quality or state of being a person. It is the amalgamation of various and distinct traits and behaviors that make up one's own personal set of characteristics.

Another definition by the American Psychological Association refers to personality as a distinct set of differences in individual thought patterns, emotion, and behavior among people.

Based on this specific meaning of the term "Personality", a person's unique set of behavioral patterns can determine key differences in personality when compared to other individuals.

The aforementioned characteristics can refer to physical, emotional, social and spiritual aspects. How can these aspects affect personality you may ask? This will be further discussed below.

The Enneagram of Personality and its Parameters

Now that we know the meaning of personality as a whole, we can move on to defining and discussing the Enneagram of Personality. This particular psychological concept refers to a basic model of the human psychological framework.

The exact term came from words of Greek origin, Ennea, and Gramma which pertains to the number 9 and anything that is illustrated by hand respectively.

This general concept refers to a set of nine different personality constructs that are intertwined and bound together in a cohesive manner by a similar foundation of traits and behavioral patterns

These constructs are normally expressed through the Enneagram figure. The main figure is basically made up of three major shapes as follows:

The Circle

This comprises the entirety of the figure. It houses the interconnected lines that represent each personality type and its similarities to one another.

The intertwining lines represent the distinctive, but related differences that each personality possesses and what each unique personality can bring to the table when it comes to interpersonal relationships.

These correlations will be discussed later in the book as part of our discussion on the motivations behind actions related to each individual personality trait.

The Inner Triangle

This connects personality types 3, 6 and 9. It also stands for the law three which according to esoteric and metaphysical beliefs represent the three basic spiritual connections: the mind, heart, and soul.

Hexagonal Shape

This particular shape represents repetition in the numerical symbols that it connects. It also symbolizes the law of seven in which there is a repeating decimal series which could be created by dividing one by seven with 10 as its base.

This particular shape represents the five aspects of personality types which can help determine the individual identity of each person.

This also shows the interconnectivity between the different personality types and how they relate to one another within the confines of the Enneagram circle.

A diagram for the Enneagram figure is seen below.

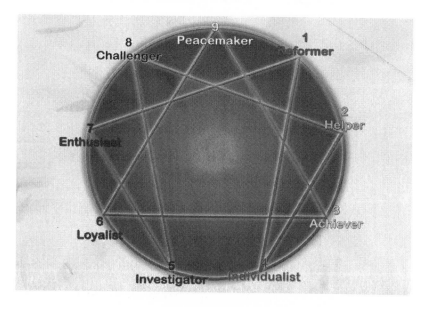

For further understanding, the five aspects of personality along with the nine Enneagram personality types will be discussed later in this particular book.

Practical Application

How can this paradigm be used as a tool for life? This is a question that can definitely help determine how the Enneagram can serve us in our daily lives.

The Enneagram works in a way that it helps us get to know the different personality types and how they ought to relate to one another.

Therefore, by comprehending the concept of the Enneagram, the readers will also understand the five aspects of personality that make up the thoughts, emotions, physical attributes and spiritual framework of an individual.

These five facets of personality determine patterns of behavior that define human identity as a whole. If one wants to understand the different personality types according to the Enneagram paradigm, he or she ought to know these five aspects of personality first.

The Main Proponents

The main concept of the Enneagram of Personality came about through the studies of Oscar Ichazo, a Bolivian-born psychologist who founded the Arica School in 1968 and Claudio Naranjo, a psychiatrist healing from Chile.

The Enneagram of Personality according to its proponents is generally part of the larger psychological concept known as Protoanalysis. This refers to a specific method of psychoanalysis developed by Ichazo himself.

This particular method of psychoanalysis examines the totality of the human being in all aspects. (Physical, Mental, Spiritual, Social, and Emotional)

Claudio Naranjo, on the other hand, is a psychiatrist that specializes in melding the process of psychotherapy with spiritual traditions. He's also one of the principal developers of the Enneagram.

Subchapter 3: The 5 Aspects of Personality in Relation to the Enneagram

The Preliminary Introduction

These distinct facets include:

- The Physical

- Emotional

- Social

- Spiritual

- Mental

These five aspects of personality work in unison to build the psychological framework of a human being.

The Enneagram of Personality basically shows the connections between these aspects as they relate to different individual traits that bring about the main flux and unique distinctions between the nine types.

Significant Effects on Personal Relationships

These five individual aspects of the personality also tend to affect the relationship-building capabilities of the nine personality types in both the positive and negative sense.

Depending on these aspects, a person can grow up to be more open to the possibility of building an external support system while still living his life in a much more reclusive manner.

Additionally, the five aspects contribute to the formation of the Enneagram because these aspects define the quality of relationships that each personality type can have as will be discussed later in this book.

How do these aspects affect interpersonal relationships as well as the Enneagram personality types? Please continue reading to learn more about it.

1. Physical

The physical appearance comprises a variety of points including the following:

- Weight

- Height
- Body type and shape
- Age
- Gender

An individual's physical appearance can affect personality in such a way that it induces certain effects on one's own perception. For example, anyone with good physical attributes tends to see themselves differently than those who are average looking.

Physical appearance lends to confidence and self-esteem which effectively helps define and shape personality as the years go by.

Physical disability can also affect individual personality in such a way that it may either make an afflicted person stronger or weaker depending on the subsequent factors to be discussed later.

Certain psychological proponents also support the role of specific body types in the formation of personality. According to various prominent psychologists, there are certain physical attributes that could directly be connected to personality. These are as follows:

A. Head Shape

A 19th-century phrenologist by the name of Franz Gall stated the idea that constructs of behavior that usually builds up the personality could be directly related to the shape of the skull.

Another renowned psychologist from the same century by the name of Cesare Lembroso said that certain physical features especially in criminals predispose them to impulsive behavior and help increase their pain threshold.

B. Body Type

20th-century German psychiatrist, Ernst Kretschmer also presented the specific classification of personality based on physical body type. These are as follows:

- **Asthenic** - This specific body type refers to those with thin, narrow-boned frames. They normally look very fragile and weak.

- **Athletic** - Muscular and energetic frames.

- **Pyknic** - Those with round and robust or large physical cavities.

- **Dysplastic** – a combination of two or more of the aforementioned body types.

According to Kretschmer, those people with any of these body types are rather susceptible to any of these two major mental disorders as follows:

Manic Depression or **Schizophrenia.**

Those with Pyknic bodies are more susceptible to becoming manic-depressive while Asthenic individuals tend to be prone to developing Schizophrenia.

This being said, Kretschmer failed to support his claims with scientific proof.

Source: Personality: Limpingco & Tria

C. Age and Gender

Age and gender also play a role in the formation of personality in terms of how an individual carries himself as a person. An older gentleman may see himself quite differently and be much more reserved than a younger lad.

The same concept applies to women. A much younger and more beautiful woman tends to have more confidence than a middle-aged lady with weight problems.

This has to do mainly with the energy and vitality that younger people have as compared to the older generation. It makes them feel that they are able to do and contribute more to society which makes them even stronger in personality.

This higher level of energy also affects the quality of relationships that younger individuals tend to cultivate with the older generation. Some older folks may find it harder to interact with the younger group because of the vast age and generational differences. The older generation may not be able to keep up with how fast-paced the modern world is.

However, with age comes wisdom as well. Knowing how to deal with certain issues because you have already lived it makes you an even more valuable member of society.

Wisdom, an integral component of the total personality, is what the younger generation lacks.

This is why it can be said that the physical appearance does not define personality in totality. There are many other facets to personality that are worth exploring in order to understand how it may be formed and cultivated in a much more positive light. Here are the other facets as follows:

2. Emotional

Emotions in the simplest sense can be defined as any conscious experience manifested through intense physical and mental reactions. It is the physical manifestation of individual reactions to certain situations and experiences in life.

This affects personality in such a way that it defines distinct behaviors exclusive to the individual depending on his or her experiences. Your emotions define your personality in such a way that it determines how you will behave when faced with either positive or negative stimuli from the environment.

3. Spiritual

Basic spirituality can be defined as one's own belief in the metaphysical entities surrounding us. It affects personality in such a way that certain behavioral patterns can occur and subsequently develop as a result of various distinct spiritual beliefs and traditions.

In some cultures, spirituality is directly linked to the shaping of individual personality so the significance of spirituality within the personality construct is something worth exploring for sure.

In this regard, the Enneagram of Personality definitely applies because it has to do with the interconnectedness of the different personality types within one mind.

It basically deals with those relationships that each individual might form with one another despite having distinct differences as mentioned earlier. This will be further discussed in the subsequent paragraphs.

In addition to this, this particular aspect of personality can directly be related to the concept of ascension and dissension in terms of human personality and evolution.

Contingent upon how spiritual person is, he or she may be able to ascend or descend to another level of personality development within the Enneagram.

Furthermore, according to the Enneagram concept, the personality types are so distinct that one cannot easily change to another type of personality altogether.

However, one personality type can achieve higher levels of existence depending on social interactions and spiritual levels that could be achieved as time passes by.

As part of the Enneagram concept, it is believed that the human personality is composed of three different centers that revolve around the core values within each personality.

The centers help each personality type evolve into a higher level of existence as mentioned earlier. What are the center's you may ask? You will find out later on in the chapter.

4. The Social Factor

Society and the related individual interactions thereof can directly affect personality because of perception. This means that individual personality as perceived by others may be contingent upon society's positive or negative opinion on certain distinct behavioral traits.

For example, personally, you may think of yourself as a fairly humble human being. However, this may change because of how others perceive you.

Depending on your relationship with people, your intrinsic perception of the self may also change.

The amalgamation of these various internal aspects and outside factors come together to form an individual construct that determines a unique set of traits that define individual perception.

These traits affect how other people interact with certain individuals and vice versa and are what you call the human personality.

5. Mental

The psychological and mental condition of each personality type can also affect personal interactions because of a difference in the belief system as well as the overall environment, culture, and traditions.

These are just a few of the external factors that can affect personal growth and development within each individual construct. It will be further discussed in the next section of the book.

External Factors that Can Affect the Enneagram and an Individual's Overall Personality Development

Now that we know the basic definition of personality and the different elements that ultimately lead to its intrinsic formation, we can now discuss the many different external factors that can affect personality development as part of the natural evolutionary cycle for humans.

Here are some of those factors as follows:

- **Traditions**

Human traditions and beliefs can also help shape personality. Depending on a person's ethnicity and basic belief system, he or she may also develop certain personality quirks related to how he perceives society as a whole.

For example, a person who grew up Catholic may behave differently than those who believe in Paganism or other eastern religions. Aside from this, subtle interactions can also put human personality in both the positive and negative light.

These are some of the reasons why personality is a beautiful thing to explore. It has many aspects that are worth seeking to understand and develop even more.

Environmental Factors and Social Interaction

Aside from the physical attributes as mentioned earlier, other factors that may affect one's developing personality are his environment and social interactions.

The place he grew up in, the people he interacts with and the overall culture of his inborn community can affect how he acts and perceives the world.

In Filipino culture, for example, they tend to stress emphasis on the importance of family. A Filipino man is raised with the belief that he has to provide for the family.

He should be the one taking care of his wife and children's basic needs as follows:

- Food

- Clothing

- Shelter

The Filipino woman, on the other hand, is tasked with handling the household. Menial chores such as cooking, cleaning the house and washing clothes are left to her care.

She is also responsible for the children's basic education prior to them being enrolled in school.

As for the family, Filipino families are known to be very close-knit. Children tend to live with their parents well into adulthood in this country and some other Asian nations.

As a result, most Filipino children tend to rely more on their parents than their own devices.

The Westerners

In the western countries, however, they focus more on independence and teaching their young how to survive on their own especially after 18 years of age.

While this is well and good because it teaches the children how to rely on themselves more, one downside of this is the fact that most western children tend to develop distance between them and their parents.

This can lead to the development of an uncaring personality for some. However, because of western independence, they learn how to fend for themselves at an early age.

Western children are known to be extremely strong willed which can be attributed to their basic culture.

Looking at the Enneagram of Personality, it can be said that personality types 5 and 8 can definitely fit the bill for individuals who are influenced by the western culture.

Personalities number four and nine fit those in the eastern culture. This being said, keep in mind that these are just as basic assessments in relation to the primary descriptions of the personalities related to the Enneagram.

Of course, there are other tests that can determine what personality type one truly has as will be discussed later on in this particular book.

If you're interested to know more about it, please do not hesitate to continue reading.

- **Religious Beliefs**

In this regard, religion also plays a role in personality development in the sense that it fosters a specific belief system that helps individuals thrive in more problematic situations.

These different types of religion and spiritual traditions can affect personality in such a way that it can help form one or more personality traits akin to the Enneagram.

For example, a person with a type 6 personality according to the Enneagram tends to have faith in a higher power, the self and others. A belief system that could have been developed by the religious construct instilled in him during childhood.

Religion can also affect personality by giving them something to aspire to. It is a great source of wisdom that could definitely shape generations of individual personality development.

My teacher once told me that religion is one way of formalizing spiritual belief. It gives tangible doctrine to what you believe in. If you have the doctrine, it will be hard it to disprove anything that you believe in.

The Importance of Human Connection in Personality Formation

The concept of personality as defined by various interpersonal relationships within one's own community and personal circle harkens back to human beings intrinsic need to relate to other people.

There are certain psychological paradigms that can explain this personal preconception.

The Oedipal and Electra Complexes

The Oedipal Complex refers to a dynamic of parental relationship wherein the child feels a strong connection towards the parent of the opposite sex while feeling resentment towards the parent of the same gender.

In this scenario, a young boy would be typically more drawn to his mother and would try to get her attention away from the father. Individuals with this kind of complex, tend to be labeled as "Mama's Boys".

This is because they do everything in their power to please their mothers and stay away from the father figure in the family.

In contrast, the Electra complex, a term coined by Carl Jung refers to a young girl's psychosexual attraction to the father.

This presents the young girl as someone who is generally thrust into a competition against the mother, ultimately vying for the father's attention.

This is where the term "Daddy's Girl" is rooted.

A person who experiences Oedipal complex tends to be more partial to the female gender. Here, men would be driven by their desire to please women as they would their mother.

It translates into a much gentler and compassionate personality for men towards women because ideally, they would not want to hurt the feelings of the opposite sex.

In contrast, men with this complex tend to be more competitive towards their own kind. They view other men as fierce rivals.

The same thing goes for women who have the Electra complex. They see their mothers as competition for their fathers' attention.

Women with this type of problem tend to want more attention from the opposite sex and would do anything and everything to get it.

Case Study:

On a personal note, I have this Christian friend who always attributes his belief in God for everything that happens in his life. He behaves the way he behaves because he believes that that is how a Christian ought to go about his life.

In contrast, an atheist friend of mine believes that he is the master of his own destiny. His personality works in such a way that every decision he makes is dependent upon what the situation calls for and not based on his intrinsic belief in the divine.

It is his belief that a higher power has nothing to do with how he behaves and how he reacts to situations. This is where the religious belief factor comes in as it relates to the formation of personality.

Some psychological experts such as Carl Jung believe that in order to fully discover the human personality one has to become self-actualized in terms of his own identity and belief system.

Jung believed that in order to achieve this goal; one has to have a steady belief system. Religion helps foster that belief.

This being said, curious minds can ask why are religion and belief such large factors in the formation of personality?

Perhaps this is because aside from being a physical body, the individual as a whole is also comprised of a spiritual being.

He or she strives to become better because he wants to have a much more improved level of existence which can only be achieved by transcending the physical plane.

This is why metaphysical concepts such as love, truth, and wisdom tend to be such profound goals for people who would like to become much more evolved versions of themselves.

This is also why failure to achieve these goals can certainly lead to feelings of worthlessness, and that reminds all manifestations of fear as illustrated in the Enneagram of Personality.

- **The Familial Upbringing: Nature vs. Nurture**

Familial upbringing is also known to play a role in the formation of personality. This works in such a way that a baby who initially does not know anything about the world is reared and taught certain behaviors all throughout infancy via different sets of processes that affect his developing psychological framework as a child.

Further proof of the effect of physical development on a child's inherent personality is Freud's related theories on sexual development in children. He purports that everyone already has sexual energy right from the beginning.

It just further develops into adulthood along with the physical attributes. Furthermore, according to Freud humans are driven by sexual desires and the need for intimacy. Everything that they do is for the satisfaction of those drives.

Now that we know what different types of situations, factors, and aspects affect personality as a whole, we can now discuss the nine personality types according to the Enneagram figure in depth.

It is our hope that the next chapter will be able to enlighten you more about the Enneagram and what it entails for the human personality as a whole. Please continue to learn more.

Chapter Two: The 9 Personality Types According to the Enneagram Figure

Reformer

A person with this personality type strives for perfection most of the time. He has a basic fear of failure and imbalance. Because of his need to be perfect, he tries to avoid situations that will lead to the corruption of his belief system as a whole.

Aside from perfection, an individual of this type of personality has three other main goals in life. This is to achieve integrity, the ultimate balance and being virtuous.

One of the downsides of his personality is that he is prone to being hypercritical of others. He also has a tendency to be a hypocrite especially if he feels the need to judge others because of their "bad behavior".

This personality type tends to be resentful of people who do not fit his idea of goodness. He also becomes extremely angered especially when he feels that he has been wronged or that someone close to him has experienced a certain type of injustice.

One outstanding quality of this type of personality is serenity. He feels very secure within himself and is not easily stressed out. He is always in control and does not let anything affect him. On the contrary, the reformer is known to be the one who affects people in a much more positive way.

This is also the reason why the Reformer is someone good to be with especially during trying times.

One should not hesitate to connect with this particular personality because you will certainly learn a lot from The Reformer. He is full of wisdom and he is not afraid to share his opinion whenever he deems it necessary.

The reformer is someone who is also extremely critical of himself. As hard as he is on others, he is doubly hard on himself in terms of expectations and discipline.

This is because he has a distinct fear of being judged himself. As mentioned earlier he strives for perfection so even the smallest mistake would be a great source of guilt for him.

As mentioned earlier, he does have a tendency to correct other people, especially in public. However, reformers do not do it to make others feel inferior.

They admonish others so that they would change for the better and become more productive members of society in the process.

If you have this particular personality type, you are lucky because you are also known to be extremely artistic. All you do is directed towards changing human perception whether of yourself or of others.

While it is good to want to see the change in other people, it is equally as important to be aware that you should be able to start the change within yourself first. Being able to influence others to change for the better will come later.

This personality type fits those individuals in leadership roles. The perfectionist qualities of this personality also fit people who would like to pay attention to detail. Designers and artists usually fall under this type.

Reformers primarily want to change the world. This is their intrinsic nature. It would be best for anyone close to them to help do this as much as possible.

If this happens, type one personalities will feel fulfilled and content that they have already lived their lives to the fullest no matter what age they are.

Positive adjectives that would describe this person would be as follows:

- Perfectionist
- Real
- Serious
- Driven

- Hardworking

Aside from those already mentioned, some of the negative aspects of this personality include:

- Judgmental
- Hypersensitive to criticism
- This personality tends to carry the weight of the world on his shoulders.
- He doesn't like to delegate because he thinks that he can do it all.
- He is extremely overconfident in himself and holds others in the same standard as himself.
- He tends to have a selfish nature at times
- He does not like being told what to do

Thought Process and Relationship Syntax: How Do You Get Along With A Reformer Type Personality?

That being said, if you would like to get along with a reformer, it would be best to be as honest as possible with this particular type of person. He cherishes the positive virtues of people.

In this regard, you have to be congenial an authentic to him.

As a reformer, a person with this particular personality type tends to want to change the individual who chooses to be connected to him for the better.

This is his main thought process. The problem with this is that most people do not want to be in a relationship to be changed. They want to be accepted for who they are. This is one of the main faults of a reformer.

Be brutally honest if you have to. Just keep telling the truth and you will get along fine with a Type 1. In addition, If you really want to be part of their inner circle it would be best for you to help them achieve their primary goal which is to be an agent of change as much as possible.

Top 5 Famous Type 1 Personalities (According to changeworks.com)

- Julie Andrews (stage and film actress, singer)
- Stephen Ambrose (historian)
- Gregory Peck (actor)
- Harrison Ford (actor)
- John Bradshaw (psychologist)

Finding Your Calling

The reformer may always find himself in situations that allow him to lead a group of people to become better members of society. If this happens, and he feels that he is happiest doing this type of service to the community, then it could be said that to lead is his calling.

Conscious Breathing Patterns and Growth Practices

The strength of their breath comes from their stomach. They have a good sense of awareness in this area of their bodies. They usually experience a lot of tension in various parts of their bodies especially if they want to do things right.

The always like to be in control which puts tension on the topmost area of their body namely the jawline, neck, and shoulders.

They usually utilize the diaphragm for breath control. There are impediments during ventilation and inhalation processes for these particular personality types.

If you have this personality type, your main goal is to make sure that you are able to relax and enjoy your breath without trying to control it. The key here is to try and let go of all your problems as you breathe.

Within the Enneagram, you must reach the point of serenity to reach the potential of your breath.

However, this may not be easy because the journey usually brings up a lot of anxiety for you. The key here is to accept the things that you cannot change so that you may be able to change the things that you can eventually.

To counteract anxiety, you should inhale through the nose and out your mouth in a much more fluid fashion. Be aware of your breath every time you do it so that you would become aware of the tension passing through your body.

Once you are able to do this, you will find more comfort when you breathe.

Then and only then can you be able to relax and be aware of your breathing. Just remember the following mantra every time you breathe. I surrender everything to something that is higher than me.

I can only control my breath everything else is secondary.

By keeping these words in your thoughts, you will be able to relax more because you will begin to let go of your fears and anxiety as you breathe in and out.

As a result, it will release your airflow and everything will be much easier down the line. You should try it as soon as possible. You will feel the effects instantly for sure.

Helper, Giver

This next specific personality type strives to exercise his free will constantly. This particular type of person is extremely open-minded and opinionated as well. This person is basically driven by the need to be loved and to love in return.

This leads to people with this personality type falling victim to false flattery most of the time.

They also have a tendency to provide false praise just to get one in return. That being said, this particular personality type is known for being extremely humble and selfless.

He or she is ready to offer help to others to the point of denying himself certain comforts in life. People with this type of personality are easily stressed and have a tendency to be insecure.

People who are fond of volunteer work fall under this type of personality. Teachers, humanitarians and the like also tend to have this type of personality.

If you have this type of personality and would like to feel growth as the helper, you should make sure that you are able to instill the value of altruism in other people.

This way, you will be able to keep the cycle going even after you are gone. It will also help you become more relevant if you are able to educate others in the art of helping people.

As the saying goes, it is important that we are able to pay it forward. You can do this by influencing others to become more like you. This is why, as mentioned earlier if people with type two personalities ought to have a career in the educative system.

This is where they would be able to do the most good.

As a helper, he is extremely sensitive to other people's emotions. This is why it can be very hard to understand him at times. Helpers can display erratic behavior especially if they are not able to do anything to help others.

In addition, it is important that helpers feel useful at all times. They want to keep busy and would feel unwell if they are not productive. If you want to be a good friend to the helper, make sure that you are able to give him something to do especially during vacant hours in the day.

This way, he will be able to exercise his creative juices much more effectively and regularly than before and share his talents with others in order to help them improve themselves in the process as well.

In addition to this, you should not hesitate to ask for help when you need it. It may be contrary to your nature but this is how you experience growth as a helper: by realizing that you need help yourself and knowing when to get it.

Positive Traits of the Helper

Aside from being altruistic, there are many other positive traits in a helper type personality. These are as follows:

- Empathic
- Thoughtful
- Understanding and available
- Selfless
- A good listener
- Daring and Bold

Negative Personality Points

- Self Deprecating
- Overly Emotional
- Has a tendency to have low self-esteem
- In some cases, this personality type seeks the approval of others to be happy.

Thought Process and Relationship Syntax: How to Get Along with Them

If you want to get along with this particular type of person, it is important that you share the same values as him. The helper gravitates towards people who are extremely charitable and will always not hesitate to share a bit of their time and energy to be of service to others.

Helpers tend to be an ideal friend and companion. The only problem with this particular personality is that they tend to want to help all the time.

They have a tendency to not let anyone else do the work. Their main thought process would be " I can do it!" which is why some people are alienated by this particular type of personality.

If you want to help out the helper, you should always be available as an assistant. He may feel that he can do everything by himself, but we all know that this is not true.

Just be there to lend a hand whenever you feel that the helper might need it.

Famous Type 2 Personalities

- Brigitte Bardot (Actress)

- Ken Burns (Filmmaker)

- Lady Diana Spencer, Princess of Wales

- Mia Farrow

- Farah Fawcett

Finding Your Calling

Type two personalities tend to find their calling in helping people. They like the feeling of being needed so they go where they could be of more use.

Volunteers, teachers and other jobs that entail public service could definitely be a fit for this type of personality.

Conscious Breathing Patterns and Growth Practices

These particular people are more into making a connection with others. Their breathing centers take energy from external forces. Those with a helping personality have the ability to empathize with others which can require more energy when it comes to breathing.

In this regard, Type 2's should breathe through the chest rather than the belly. They also usually hold their breath while waiting for responses from other stimuli.

If you have this type of personality, it is important that you look inside yourself to examine your own feelings and sensations.

In terms of the Enneagram, your main goal is to reach a point of personal humility. You feel safe and secure in this feeling.

You have to be able to separate your own feelings from those of others.

You also have to focus on yourself once in a while so that you can give more. As the saying goes, how can you love somebody else if you can't even try to love yourself first?

Achiever or Performer

This personality type is known for being hopeful and law-abiding. He strives to be as honest as possible in any particular situation. People with this type of personality wants to feel valuable and has a fear of being worthless and losing the attention of the public.

This is why he or she always strives to do his best in everything that the person tackles. He or she will do everything in their power to achieve the goal that they set for themselves even if they sacrifice their health for it.

These performing types of individuals are known to be vain as well. They have a tendency to keep up appearances and be deceitful in order to hide their personal weaknesses.

This leads to them being easily stressed out by simple things. They also tend to be easily defeated by things not going their way. If you have this kind of personality, it would help you to be honest with yourself as much as possible.

This way, you will not have additional problems to deal with down the line.

Most of the time, achievers tend to believe their own hype regarding how good they are. If you are an achieving type of personality, it is important to try to keep your feet on the ground as much as possible. Then and only then can you achieve true greatness.

Try to spend an equal amount of time by yourself facing the mirror. This way, you will be able to introspective and see yourself and your motivations for what they really are. Doing this will help you become more honest with yourself and with others down the line.

Film, stage actors and performers usually have this predominant personality type. Anyone who likes to seek attention tends to have this personality as well.

These types the people should be careful to let the fame go into their heads. Otherwise, they will end up destroying themselves and other people around them.

They are at their own worst enemy so to speak so they have to be extremely careful about the choices that they make

As an achiever, it would be good to surround yourself with people who will be honest with you even if most individuals tell you what you want to hear. This way, you will not end up being overconfident in having a huge ego.

If you have this type of personality, it would help you to make being humble your goal in life. Once you are able to achieve this, you will feel much better about yourself and others for sure.

You should perform to make other people happy and not the other way around. This way, you will still have the humility in your heart amidst the fame and recognition that he will surely get for your performances and achievements in the days to come.

So what do you think? Are you an achiever or more of a follower? Either way, it is important for you to be humble always. You will feel much more fulfilled as a type three personality this way.

Positive Traits

- Artistic
- Confident
- Wants to be at his best always
- Strives to improve in every area of his life

Negative Traits

- Attention-seeking
- Selfish
- Insensitive to other people's feelings

Thought Process and Relationship Syntax

To connect, one has to be able to make the achiever feel good about himself. This particular type of personality likes attention. So if you want to get along with him or her, it is important that you are able to provide him with the attention that he needs.

This particular type tends to be more of a "me" person. They think that everything that happens should revolve around them. They see the attention of others because they want to be seen.

They handle personal relationships in such a way that they connect with people because they would get something out of it.

This being said, however, you also have to make sure that he is able to hear what he has to hear in order to keep his feet on the ground. Performers and achievers tend to have a grandiose view of themselves.

This is why you have to be the one to keep them in check if you are going to be their friend.

In addition, do not be intimidated by their strong personalities. Achievers tend to have a much more dominant personality than most. This is why they are able to go to such great heights in their chosen field.

If you are to be their friend, it is important that you have your own sense of self. You have to be confident in who you are so that you won't be easily intimidated and envious by your achiever friend's success.

Be comfortable in your own skin and you will be able to interact with an achiever much more smoothly than any other person.

Renowned Type Three Personalities

- Muhammad Ali
- Tony Blair
- Lance Armstrong
- David Copperfield
- Danielle Steele

Finding Your Calling

Performers and achievers tend to find satisfaction in gaining the attention of others. They like being in the center stage to be seen by others. This is their main calling in life.

If you feel that you have the type 3 personality, it would be best for you to choose a career path that aligns with the performing arts.

Conscious Breathing Patterns and Growth Practices

With this particular type of personality, breathing is centered towards wanting to please others. They are extremely lively and energetic. This is why it can be quite a challenge for them to silently examine their feelings and their breath.

If you have this type of personality, it is important that you are able to slow down and practice breathing by turning your attention inward. This will allow you to be aware of your inner self and what your motivations are.

It will help you discover your real intentions and priorities in life so that you can live in full awareness of your surroundings.

The main goal is to reach a point of truthfulness and authenticity within yourself. Your breathing tends to be centered on your chest where there's also a lot of energy.

Individualist

This particular personality type is also known as the Romantic. Anyone with this personality type always strives to find his purpose in life. He wants to understand where he comes from and where he's going.

People with this type of personality tend to daydream and use their imagination a lot. They have their own world in their mind which sometimes affects their view of reality.

His greatest fear is to not have a sense of identity and a significant role in the world. This is why he strives to find his purpose. One downside of having this personality is that this particular individual tends to be envious of others who have better lives compared to him.

Being idealistic, he does not realize that everybody has their own problems and thinks that life is just something to be enjoyed. This is also a plus for him because an individualist tends to be more emotionally balanced and mature.

He is able to persevere through hard times because of his imaginative nature.

However, he tends to go into deep melancholy ones things don't go his way. He tends to withdraw and become more of a recluse. If left unchecked, this distorted view of life will lead to his fear of abandonment and self-assertion.

If one wants to interact with an individualist, he or she should be reminded that this particular individual has a different sense of reality than most. He or she should be what willing to share in the individualist's dreams while still making an effort to keep their feet on the ground.

Writers and artists usually have this type of personality. They tend to use their imaginations often and are not rooted in reality when it comes to their thoughts.

If you have this type of friend, just leave them be if they have their episodes. They just need some time to let their creative juices flow and will come back to reality once they work it out.

On the other hand, if you have this type of personality, you have to be careful not to let your fantasy world distort your view of reality.

Type four personalities should be able to develop a strong sense of focus to keep themselves from becoming swept away by their own dreams and thoughts.

It would help to have a reliable support system such as the family or friends to help an individualist retain a sense of who he truly is as a person.

This way, he will be able to go through life without regrets because of any missed chances and opportunities down the line.

An individualist also tends to become more of the dreamer than the realist. If you have this type of personality, it is important that you are able to reconcile the difference between a dream and an attainable goal.

This way, you will have more chances of achieving what you want without getting distracted in the process.

You should also make it a point to have a visual representation of your plan. This way, you will not have difficulty getting a sense of where you were and where you want to go in life.

Having a plan helps you figure out how you will reach your goal right from the beginning. This way of thinking and directional approach in life will surely make things easier for you down the line.

It is not too difficult to be an individualist. Just make sure that you have a strong sense of reality while still being a romantic at heart. Try to be as grounded as you possibly can, but still keep hoping your heart especially during challenging situations.

If you can do this, then you will not have a hard time navigating your life with this personality type as part of your identity as a complete and mature individual.

Positive Characteristics of Type 4 Personalities

- Creative
- Artistic
- Imaginative

Negative Characteristics

- Detached from Reality
- Limited by His or Her Fear

- Has a tendency to become dependent because of his fear of abandonment.

Thought Process and Relationship Syntax

If you want to be friends with this particular type of personality, it is important that you are able to understand his or her thought process first.

These particular personalities are not serious types. They always live in a fantasy world and would most likely want to always be flippant about things.

As a friend, you have to be cordial and accommodating with the romantic. Be open to listening to his or her ideas, but also try to keep her feet on the ground.

This way, she will see you as an invaluable friend who will always be there to help her out no matter what.

In addition, an individualist thinks of everything as fantasy. Because of this, this particular person tends to strive for a happy ending. He or she has an unrealistic view of the world and would come crashing down once he is faced with the harsh reality of life.

In terms of relationships, this particular personality type is a good friend to have because he will always see the good in you. However, individualists can be very sensitive and will not be able to handle brutal honesty.

Famous Type 4's

- John Barrymore
- Angelina Jolie
- Michael Jackson
- James Dean
- Janis Joplin

Finding Your Calling

If you are more of an individualist or a romantic, this means that you like being alone most the time. You find solace in being alone with your thoughts. You are more creative when you work alone so this could be your calling.

Find a career that would require you to spend all your energies on one project by yourself.

The creative arts such as writing, painting, and designing usually derives fulfillment from the talents of the individual himself. This personality type will develop more if he is able to hone his talents and achieve its goals without external assistance.

Conscious Breathing Patterns and Growth Practices

These particular individuals have intense feelings and emotions that tend to bring them up or down most of the time. They are concerned with forging meaningful external relationships with others.

They also go back and forth between wanting to receive recognition and retreating into their own little world.

Their breathing patterns are known to be tied to their emotions. This means that depending on their emotional state, their breath might be erratic and shallow as well.

Deep breathing exercises are advised for the individualist especially if their emotions are heightened. This will calm them down right away.

You must breathe into the nose and out of the mouth. Feel your breath flow through you as you breathe in and out. This way, you will feel your energy come back to you as you apply these exercises. Do this for about 10 minutes or so without stopping.

Investigator

The investigator is known to be a keen observer as well. He's extremely honest and transparent in his feelings and emotions towards others. This is also what he strives for.

He wants to know the truth about each and every individual and situation.

A person with this particular personality type does not like to feel helpless and incapable of doing things on his own. He also hates incompetence in himself and in others.

He strives for knowledge, mastery, and understanding of all things.

In this regard, anyone with this particular set of personality traits tends to focus more on individual concepts rather than the whole experience. In short, he thinks more than he does.

Because of this, he has a tendency to want to take all the credit for himself. He wants to have everything and does not like to share. He tries to do everything by himself and would not want to become attached and indebted to other people.

He also has a love for puzzles and mysteries to be solved. An investigator tends to be very inquisitive especially about things that are new and foreign to him.

Try not to be involved in a debate with this particular personality type. Otherwise, you will find yourself with no escape. It is important to the investigator that everyone around him is honest about who they are because he has an aversion towards lying.

If you are not your authentic self when spending time with an investigator, chances are you will have a hard time connecting with him. It is important that you maintain a semblance of openness and honesty with investigators.

Similarly, if you have a friend with this type of personality, be prepared for unbridled frankness. He will not be afraid to share his thoughts with you so you should not be too sensitive. You should be ready to help but wait for him to ask. He is not ready to accept defeat so always try to be gentle in your admonitions of your investigator friend.

Just like the reformer, this particular personality type would be much needed in a leadership position. He will be able to tell people what to do and direct them accordingly as to where they should put their efforts much more intensely.

Police officers and those in law enforcement also fit the bill when it comes to having this particular type of personality. They like giving focus on the minute details and give emphasis on the whys of actions rather than the action itself.

If you have this type of personality, law enforcement is the job for you. Just make sure that you are well prepared for the challenges ahead. Do not be afraid to use your inquisitiveness to your own advantage.

You will not regret your decision to enter law enforcement as a five. Your love for adventure and mysteries will suit you well in this field.

Fives tend to have coldness as part of their personality trait. However, once you are able to break through their defenses, they will become a loyal friend and fierce companion. This is why you should not hesitate to become a friend of this particular personality type.

They also feel much aversion to protectors in terms of the Enneagram. This may be because they have similar characteristics as people. However, while these personalities may clash at first, eventually given some time they will learn to like each other and become good friends.

On the other hand, if you have an individualistic personality, you will find herself drawn to the investigator mainly because of his curious nature. Individualists tend to be fantastical in their thoughts which the investigator can find extremely interesting.

Do you have similar personality traits to the investigator? Do you think it's an advantage or disadvantage? Here are some more positive and negative traits of the investigator so as to help you clear things even more.

Positive Traits

- Analytical
- Strong and Independent
- Curious
- Inquisitive
- Persistent
- Always after the truth
- Never gives up

Negative Traits

- Stubborn
- Always wants to have his way
- Forceful at times

Thought Process and Relationship Syntax

The investigative personality prides itself in being independent and curious. If you have the same characteristics, chances are you will find solace in each other's company.

Investigators tend to be more analytical problem solvers so if you truly want to be friends with them, it is important that you are able to capture their interest the moment that you need for the first time.

As mentioned earlier, it has similar characteristics to the first personality type which is a reformer. This is why if you are a helper or the peacemaker, you will most likely have an easier time connecting with this particular personality type.

This personality's thought process goes something like, "everything is a mystery that has to be solved." He is wary of people who want to connect with him; a trait which makes this personality not very easy to connect with.

However, once he does connect with people, he will certainly be the best friend you will ever have.

Famous Icons with Fifth Personality Type

- Bobby Fischer (Chess)
- Bill Gates
- Greta Garbo

- Stephen Hawking

- Alfred Hitchcock

Finding Your Calling

Investigators and observers tend to get satisfaction from finding out key pieces of information. They live for solving mysteries and finding answers to difficult questions.

People with this type of personality have a calling to try and surmount seemingly impossible odds.

Police officers and detectives tend to be aligned with this particular personality type. They will be able to find growth and development if they are able to hone their investigative skills and help others while doing it.

Conscious Breathing Patterns and Growth Practices

The investigator is known to be an extremely thoughtful person. He mainly seeks to develop himself and his expertise while protecting others and his own privacy. These types of personalities require a lot of personal space.

Fives are more detached and then the normal human being. They seem to be cold when interacting with others as well. However, this is just because of their being thoughtful and introspective.

If you are one of those investigative personalities, it would help you to establish a connection with your body as well as your emotions. These types of personalities tend to hold their breath in order to avoid sensation and feeling.

However, this is not advisable. Holding your breath will constrict your energy flow and deplete your vitality.

It will prevent you from connecting with others because you will remain trapped in your head thinking about what other people might say. You need to connect with others in order to access the energy of your instincts.

By doing this, you will definitely increase your pleasure centers and the sensations that they release.

In order to develop your body and breathing further, it would be best to take deep breaths from the diaphragm. It may cause you to be anxious at first, but eventually, it will be good for your health and growth as a human being.

Loyalist

This particular personality type delves more into belief in the self and others. It works around the idea that there is always a higher power at work within the personality construct.

As a result, an individual with this particular personality construct tends to depend on the higher power and others of more authority than himself. This is why the loyalist is known to be much more spiritual than all the other personality types apart from the Peacemaker.

He always attributes his successes and failures to a God-Given skill or talent that he has.

Because of this, he always has a constant fear of being alone. He is prone to being indecisive, having self-doubt and always seeking reassurance from others.

That being said, his belief in himself and in people around him tends to give him enough courage to go on and live his life to the fullest.

He always wants to be well-liked because he thrives in being surrounded by supportive individuals who believe in him as much as he believes in them.

This is also one of the downsides to this personality type because it gives the loyalist the tendency to become a people pleaser. The loyalist also tends to be blind to criticism against his or her friends.

He refuses to hear reason when it comes to negative opinions regarding the people he feels closest to.

Because of this, he has a tendency to be tricked much more easily than other personality types. He is easily convinced by someone who shows him any goodwill.

He does not want to be as confrontational especially to a friend. He will give you the benefit of the doubt a thousand times before letting go of the friendship.

Being a friend of a loyalist will definitely help boost your own confidence. They will always be there for you no matter what. However, you have to be very careful about exercising fish your own independence when it comes to the relationship.

These people tend to be dependent on their friends. Make sure to be firm, but kind when it comes to explaining that you need your independence as well. Try to not be always there. This way, he will learn to not depend on you too much but rely on his own devices as well.

This being said, once he does let go of the friendship he will never come back. This is because he is known to spend all his energy helping and loving his friends to the point that he sometimes forgets himself already. So once he lets you go that's the end of it for sure.

Once you earn their trust, it will be with you for life. However, if you by any chance break it for any reason, it will be very hard for them to trust you again. They may even turn your other friends against you.

He's willing to fight for a friend but is not willing to confront his friends when they do him wrong. This still goes to the pleasing tendency that tends to develop within a loyalist personality.

Ultimately, the loyalist is a good friend to have. As mentioned earlier, you just have to make sure that you are honest about your feelings towards him and towards the people around him.

You will certainly reap the benefits of a strong friendship with this personality type in the end. You should definitely get a loyalist friend right away. You will not regret it one bit for sure.

Outstanding Characteristics

- Trusting
- Always sees the good and people
- Understanding
- Faithful

Negative Characteristics

- Blind to Criticism about Friends
- Indecisive

Thought Process and Relationship Syntax

If you would like to truly get along with this particular personality type, it is important that you are able to respect his or her beliefs. Do not try to persuade him into your way of thinking right off the bat.

As a friend, it is your duty to be able to communicate with him or her in a respectful manner that will not infringe upon his or her freedoms as an individual.

In addition to this, you should also try your best to be worthy of the loyalist's trust.

A loyalist is someone who will be there for you no matter what happens. So make sure that as a friend, you will do everything in your power to be worthy of that kind of love and loyalty.

A loyalist values his or her support system above all else. He tries his best to be liked so that he will have people surrounding him all the time. This particular personality type can be seen as extroverted. He takes his energies from other people and thrives in a group.

His thought process always centers on what others might think of him which can be mistaken for wanting to please others. In truth, this person only just values the support system that other people can afford him.

Be honest about your feelings and you will be rewarded by this particular personality type with years of strongly bonded friendship.

Well-Known 6's

- Jason Alexander
- Woody Allen
- President George H.W. Bush
- Tom Clancy
- Lynda Carter

Finding Your Calling

People with type six personalities tend to be good followers. They are good with instructions and are able to execute them well. Homemakers and employees tend to have this type of personality.

If you are one of these you should definitely choose a career path that will allow you to serve people better. This way, you will be able to find more fulfillment and personality development down the line.

Conscious Breathing Patterns and Growth Practices

Type six personalities are extremely perceptive individuals. They can anticipate problems and find solutions effectively. They are known to be a stickler for rules and find comfort and security and procedural behavior.

If you are one of those sixth personality types, you should take slow and deep breaths in order to expand your diaphragm and release tension as much as possible.

Take time exhaling so as to relax your body and mind while being aware of your breath. This will provide more energy to handle the difficulties that may come your way.

As part of your breathing and growth practice, make sure that you are able to breathe through your chest whenever you feel worry or anxiety. This will help you steady your breath and think clearly as you journey through your life in the long run.

Enthusiast

This particular personality type is known to be the planner of the group. He is full of life experience and wisdom that he uses to help others along the way.

His main goal in life is to become satisfied and content. If you encounter a person with this personality type, you will most likely deal with someone who is always trying to find fulfillment.

His greatest fear is being deprived of overall satisfaction in life which leads to wanting to take it all in. He tends to be a glutton for everything good in life.

This is why he wants to do everything at once. He rarely says no to a challenge as well. He will try everything in its power to achieve this goal even if it seems insurmountable.

The enthusiast tends to be interested in many things at once. This is why he has a tendency to not follow through with everything that he promises. He tends to be distracted a lot because he wants to do everything all at once.

He has a lot of pent-up energy but does not know how to spend it wisely. This is one of the reasons why he tends to fall short on some of the things that he wants to do.

Connecting with the enthusiast is something that can be very challenging for some people. This holds true especially if they cannot match the energy level that the enthusiast usually puts out.

If you would like to have a meaningful relationship with this type of personality, it would be best to find out what you have in common and focus on those commonalities. This way, you will find that he will be the one to gravitate towards you more so than before.

The enthusiast is a good friend to have because he will help you truly get out of your comfort zone. However, you also have to rein him in sometimes. Be the one to ground the enthusiast. If you can do this effectively, he will appreciate you more as a friend for sure.

These are just some of the main characteristics of the seventh personality type also known as The Enthusiast. Below are some more character traits that you should know.

If you really want to connect with this particular personality, be ready for quite an adventure. It will certainly not be boring to have this particular personality type in your life.

You may even be influenced by him as time goes by. Hopefully, it will all turn out great in the end for the enthusiastic types.

Positive Traits

- Energetic
- Courageous
- Daring
- Fun
- Strong Willed

Negative Traits

His strong will and his inability to see the danger of what he wants to do more often than not the same into trouble. He should have someone in his life who will keep him in line.

Thought Process and Relationship Syntax: How to Get Along with an Enthusiast

If you want to get along with this particular personality type, you have to be willing to enjoy his company. This means that you would have to join him in whatever type of adventure he has in store for the day.

The enthusiast will not get along with anyone who tries to stop him from doing what he does to enjoy his life.

His target is always to find wisdom in everything he touches. Everything he does is for this one goal. This thought crosses centers on his willingness to grow as a person through knowledge. This is why he is willing to try everything.

His relationships revolve around the same aspect. If he feels that he can learn from you and vice versa, he will be glad to connect and become friends.

As a friend, remind him of the pros and cons of what he is about to do. This way, he will be aware of the consequences and will have an informed decision regarding the possible effects.

Be there for him always, but tried to steer him down the right path as much as you can. Do not stand idly by if you feel that he's doing anything that will harm others or himself. Being a good friend means calling him out when he is wrong.

The Enthusiast type needs to realize that not everything is fun and games. If you want to be a good friend to him, you should make him realize this right away. In short, always be a good influence.

Famous Sevens

- Tim Allen
- Chevy Chase
- Cher
- George Clooney
- Billy Crystal

Finding Your Calling

The enthusiasts tend to be interested in many different things. Ultimately, he wants to be satisfied and live a full life. This is why he tries his best to give everything a shot.

He feels inadequate and fees unable to live out his full potential if he is confined to a single space. If you find yourself wanting to travel the world and touching other people's lives as you go along, then this is your calling.

You will find further personality development if you are able to do everything that you want to do at the moment.

Conscious Breathing Patterns and Growth Practices

This particular personality type is known to have a creative mind. They are known to explore all options and are good and having fun. Of all the personality types, the Enthusiasts are known to be great at handling massive amounts of information at one time.

They handle stimuli extremely well and have heightened sensory perception.

If you are one of these enthusiastic types, it is important that you are able to be in touch with your feelings. If you feel displaced or imbalanced, just search yourself and be aware of how you feel at the moment.

This may be boring at first but once you get used to it, you will be able to increase your self-awareness and use it to calm yourself down whenever necessary.

Using your stomach as a center for breathing will help you achieve being grounded and increase physical sensation in your lower body. When you feel detached to your physical body because of worry or fear, just practice breathing into your stomach on a regular basis.

You can also lie on your belly and straighten your feet and legs while doing this breathing exercise. This will help you achieve greater results in terms of relaxation and self-discovery for growth.

Challenger or Protector

Anyone with this personality type is driven by the need to take care of themselves. They are known to be self-sufficient and would not rely on others for help. People with this particular personality type focuses mainly on self-improvement so as to become reliable to others.

One of the negative aspects of these individuals is that they tend to be focused on themselves more than others. These people tend to be extremely selfish and forceful in their ways.

They always try to get what they want and will do everything in their power to have it. On a more positive note, however, they always think about other people's welfare first and would be willing to give up their own life to protect others if worse comes to worst.

People in positions of power such as presidents, chief executive officers of companies and top law enforcement posts tend to have this type of personality.

Whether they have it innately or if the situation calls for it is entirely debatable. However, this is what the situation and the job entails. As a challenger, it is important that these people are able to rise to the occasion when need be.

This is why it is good for them to be in positions of power and leadership. It allows them to become in control of their environment in a much more conducive away.

Challengers always want to be ahead. As mentioned earlier, they do not like rely on other people for help which is why it would be hard for anyone to connect with them on a more personal level.

However, that they do let people who have proven themselves to be reliable and trustworthy in their circle.

If you are one of those people, then you are in luck because once the challenger lets you in, he will be the most fears protector that you can have as a friend. He will even take anyone closest to you under his wing.

This is where the protective side of this particular personality type comes out. He is extremely protective of his family and loved ones which is why he's the most important person to have in your life. You just have to be ready to face his strong personality which can sometimes be borderline domineering.

Otherwise, you will not look for any other person to rely on if you have a challenger by your side. This being said, please be careful about connecting with challengers.

They can be difficult to work with or connect to at first, but once you get to know them, you will realize just how sensitive of a soul they could be.

So what are you waiting for? Go ahead and try to connect with a challenger right now. I am sure that you will not have any regrets if you ever decide to do so. It will be one of the best decisions that you will have made in your life for sure.

Positive Traits

- Strong mind and character
- Usually physically fit
- Doesn't easily falter
- Independent-minded
- Go-getter

Negative Traits

- Obstinate
- Overprotective
- Not a very good listener

Thought Process and Relationship Syntax: Getting Along with a Challenger

If you want to be a friend to the challenger, it is important that you are able to let this personality take the lead. Share your opinion but ultimately let him decide for himself what he wants to do.

This way, he will see you as an invaluable source for help or advice whenever necessary.

Speaking of advice, you should also try to let him come to you for help instead of forcing yourself on him. Challengers do not like to be told what to do whether by friends or by an authority figure.

If they need help, they will ask for it, which is why you need to always be available for this type of friend.

He is driven by thoughts of wanting to protect people. This can also border around vengeance. This is why people with this personality type have to be careful about harboring ill feelings towards another person.

However, if his motivations are clear, everything will work out great for someone with a type 8 personality.

Relationship-wise, being that the personality is driven by protecting people, he is also drawn to the weak and oppressed. If you're someone in need of protection or is very dependent in nature, then type 8 personalities will be drawn to you.

If you feel that he needs help and yet he doesn't want to ask for it still, you have to make and realize that he does need you. A good friend to the challenger means someone who doesn't nag him and yet is always present in his life whenever you need to be.

It is important that you are able to give them the space that he needs to think while still being there for counsel whenever he needs it.

Personality Type Eight: Famous Icons

- Michael Douglas
- Morgan Freeman
- Indira Gandhi

- Theodore Roosevelt

- Shaquille O'Neal

Finding Your Calling

This particular personality type likes seemingly difficult challenges. He is able to rise above every problem and deal with it head-on. If you have this type of personality, chances are like the reformer, you are called to become a leader.

People like these help individuals who try to help themselves. Doctors, teachers, and action-oriented individuals tend to find fulfillment when they are able to face challenges head-on. If you find yourself wanting to be in these particular fields, then it is most likely that this is your calling.

Conscious Breathing Patterns and Growth Practices

Type eight personality based individuals are extremely assertive. They have open access to their instincts which makes them more intuitive than most. If you have the character traits of a challenger, it would be best to relax and show vulnerability despite being in a leadership position.

This may cause you some anxiety and fear but it will yield a lot of advantages if you are able to keep up the practice. It will open you up emotionally and develop your empathic senses.

Do not be afraid to connect with others if ever you find yourself needing help. Once you are able to open yourself up, people will certainly gravitate toward you and your company.

In return, you will have more energy to live your life and grow as an individual. As for your breathing, it is important that you are able to manage your breath depending on the situation at hand.

Try to avoid breathing through your chest as this will gather strong energies and heighten your emotions. Instead, when confronted with tension-filled situations, practice deep breathing to help you relax.

Be aware of your breathing direction as you go up and down. This will help you think clearly and in a much more mature manner so as to handle the situation properly.

Peacemaker and Mediator

This last type deals with those who are extremely calm in personality. They always have a tendency to daydream and neglect the basic realities of life. Their goal in life is to achieve wholeness and peace of mind in whatever way possible.

These individuals tend to operate with the idea that they are worthy of being loved and loving in return. This being said, their idea of love is more a romanticized version of the concept rather than the real thing.

They are not ready to sacrifice everything that they have for someone else because they would rather live in an ideal world of peace and harmony.

They are afraid of getting lost and being separated from other people, especially from the ones that they love. They try to avoid conflicts and self-assertion in every situation. They like it when other people decide for them.

This being said, the main virtue of this personality is action. They always want to do something in their mind but lack the courage and conviction to enact their plans. Their main goal is to have peace and quiet in their lives.

If you have this particular personality type, then it is important for you to achieve an ultimate sense of well-being. You are averse to getting hurt and hurting others as well. You always advocate for peace.

This is a good thing, but the problem lies with you and not being able to take action about anything that you would want to do in your life.

Nines are good advice givers, but, more often than not; do not know how to take their own advice. This is because they have a tendency to become reclusive in prayer and contemplation always.

They have a tendency to be trapped inside their heads with concepts of goodness and their will to change the world but when it comes to taking action, they will not have enough courage to do so.

They are extremely quiet and revel in their own thoughts. This is why if you would want to connect with the ninth personality type, it would be best for you to connect with them emotionally. Open yourself up and be willing to share your thoughts and feelings with them.

They will be a good person to discuss your spiritual beliefs with. You may not agree about things all the time, but these nines are extremely open-minded and will not judge you for who you are and what you believe in no matter how outlandish your theories are about life.

What is important to them is that they have someone to connect to. If you are able to do this for them, they will cherish your presence in their lives and even allow you to partake in their contemplation and prayer.

This will be a great opportunity for you to explore your own spirituality. The peacemaker will be a good guide and confidant, particularly in these matters. It will be a symbiotic relationship as they will help you find yourself while you are helping them connect with the outside world.

Below are some of the positive and negative traits that you can look forward to if you ever decide to interact with the peacemaker. Take a look at them and see if you have any of these particular traits.

Positive Traits

- Humble

- Unassuming

- Quiet

- Contemplative

- Enduring

Negative Traits

Self Sacrificial – He puts the needs of others before himself so much that it becomes a danger to his own health.

Thought Process and Relationship Syntax: How to Get Along with the Peacemaker

If you want to get along with the peacemaker, you have to be able to listen to what he has to say. Join him in meditation and prayer as much as you can.

Always try to be his source of inspiration as a friend. This way, you will be able to give them the help that he needs whenever he feels at a loss.

It would also help to become his confidant from time to time. This way, you will be able to boost his confidence whenever necessary.

You will also be able to give some solace whenever there's a problem and help them out in times of need.

This last personality type focuses on wanting to gain the love of the people surrounding him. His thought processes mainly revolve around peace and tranquility. He always wants to relax and be worry-free.

He never likes conflict with other people. This is why he always seeks to have harmonious relationships wherever he goes. Type nine personalities are extremely non-confrontational in nature.

Always be available whenever he needs someone to talk to. If you are able to do this, then you will have succeeded in becoming a good friend to the peacemaker.

Famous Type 9's

- Jennifer Aniston
- Kofi Annan
- Oscar De La Renta
- Nancy Kerrigan
- Luke Perry

Finding Your Calling

As mentioned earlier, these types of personalities find fulfillment in wanting to facilitate connections. They find satisfaction in helping others become better versions of themselves through introspection.

These individuals normally have a calling for priesthood or the monastery.

Conscious Breathing Patterns and Growth Practices

Peacemakers are generally intuitive in nature. This is why they feel sensitive towards anything foreign and new. In order to grow properly, it is important that these personality types are able to go out of their comfort zone and get in on the action.

Do not be afraid to take on difficult tasks if it will further improve your own self in the process. Peacemakers are known to have more time to get things done because they spend most of their time contemplating and communicating with a higher power.

This is why it will be a perfect time to take action and step out of the familiar territory.

If you are the nine, use your breath to become more aware of your body, mind, and emotion. You have the ability to tap into spiritual guidance more so than others.

This way, you will also be able to create boundaries that can help you be aware of what you need instead of what you want. Knowing yourself will allow you to not be easily swayed by other people's opinions and therefore help you grow as an individual and as a member of the community.

Additional Information

These are the nine personality types that are interconnected in a way that describes the entirety of the personality. If one or more characteristics go dormant in these particular personality types, it would definitely result in dire consequences for the subject himself.

The Enneagram of Personality purports that the whole individual is not comprised of a single type of personality but an amalgamation of different traits that make up the human psyche. It just so happens that one or more of these personality traits is far more evident than others.

This being said, the Enneagram of personality also states that one personality type cannot evolve into another personality type within the parameters of the figure. They can only improve within the parameters of the specific personality types.

For example, a type one personality (reformer) will not be able to turn into a type 5 (investigator). However, these personality types can reach their individual goals in life as mentioned above. This means that the peacemaker can achieve great love in his life.

The reformer can get to his version of perfection and the achiever can learn to value himself through the events that will transpire in his lifetime.

This is how and why the various personality types emerged; distinct, but always interconnected.

Discovering One's Specific Enneagram Personality Type and How Behavior Modification Can Play a Role in Improving These Constructs

In this section, we will help you discover how you can find out for yourself with your personality type is contingent upon the Enneagram of Personality discussed earlier. What are the steps that you can take to achieve this?

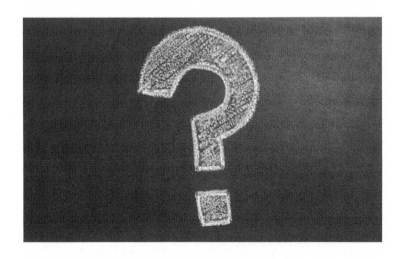

In addition, we will also discuss how you can get to change any negative aspects of your personality through various behavior modification techniques. Please continue reading to learn more about some helpful advice that you can take with regards changing your own personality for the better.

Part One: Simple Steps That You Can Take To Find Out Your Very Own Enneagram Personality Type

As discussed earlier, the Enneagram of Personality is composed of nine different types. These types have different ways by which they approach life and simple thought.

Once you discover what your personality type truly is, It will be easy for you to understand your basic motivations for displaying such distinct behavioral patterns.

However, how will you be able to do this? What steps can you take to discover the kind of personality that you have according to the Enneagram? Here are some of the steps as follows:

There is a test available online that will help you discover your own personality type by answering a series of questions with regards your recent behavior and tendencies.

If you do not want to take the online test, you can go back to our list of different personality types according to the Enneagram, read it again and determine if the descriptions in this particular section of the book apply to you.

Here is a link to the online tests that you can take.

After you are able to discover your personality type you can easily discover what personality wing you belong to. The wings will determine the kind of interactions you may end up having with different types of personalities depending on the elements within your own construct.

In reference to the Enneagram figure, the wings refer to the adjacent points representing the different personalities in the figure. For instance, in the picture, you can see that the second type of personality has one and 3 on either side of the figure.

This means that personalities one and three can both negatively and positively affect the second set of personality.

To illustrate, personality 1 (the Reformer) can help personality 2 (the Helper) improve his or her quality of service by showing him a better way of helping people. Perhaps instead of giving them fish, the reformer can convince the helper to teach them how to fish.

On the other hand, someone with the mediating or peacemaking personality can have a harmonious relationship with the enthusiast because they both want contentment and peace of mind. It is important to remember that various personalities to interact differently to a situation depending on a variety of factors as follows:

- Their thought process
- Past Experiences
- Motivation and drive
- Overall belief system

This is where the Enneagram of Personality can help a person discover how he thinks and what other people might see in him.

The Enneagram will help you understand the world around you in such a way that you will be able to pinpoint the main cause of certain human behaviors down the line.

This particular concept is all about self-observation and the observation of the world around you. If you are able to do this, then you will get to develop your personality even faster than ever before.

Part 2: Instincts and Personality

According to the Enneagram of Personality, an individual has three different personality subtypes or motivations for behaving a certain way. These are as follows:

- **Sexual -** The sexual instinct has to do with how one person deals with a partner in an intimate sense.

- **Social -** This particular instance deals with how one person interacts with a group of people.

- **Self -** According to this particular instinctual motivation, an individual has an innate desire to protect himself and think only of his needs above others.

These three instinctual motivators are what drive people to form their behavioral patterns that usually determine the specific personality types. If you want to change intrinsically, you have to discover what your basic instinct is and how you are motivated by it in terms of behavior.

What Will You Do When You Discover Your Type?

It is one thing to discover more about your personality type in terms of the Enneagram. However, it is another entirely different issue as to what you should do after you discover it.

This section will deal with how you can reconcile your personality type with what you are already doing with your life at present.

By reading this section, we hope that you will be able to understand yourself more as well as your motivations for doing what you are doing right now. If you want to learn more about what you should do, do not hesitate to read on. You will surely learn a lot.

To answer the first question, it really depends on the specific number that your personality belongs to in the Enneagram. Here is a list as follows:

1. Reformers

If you discover yourself as a reformer, then you know that your main weakness is resentment and you fear corruption, not being balanced and lacking morality. To change this, you can re-evaluate your values.

Why are you doing good things for people? Are you doing it for yourself or truly to help others? Always remember that doing the right things for the wrong reasons is not very healthy.

You have to do something because you want to do it. Not because you want something in return. By keeping this in mind, your motivations for helping others and living your life will align with the right path.

2. Helpers

As mentioned earlier, your basic fear is to be unloved by others. To counteract this, you have to make sure that you continue helping those in need.

Remember the golden rule of Confucius. Do unto others as you would want others to do unto you. If you give love to the world, it will come back to you a hundred times more. You will not have to worry about being unloved any longer.

3. The Achiever

For achievers and performers, your main concern and fixation would be vanity. According to the Enneagram, you do not like feeling worthless. To rid of these feelings, you have to be able to keep your feet on the ground.

Always remember that the attention people give you, whether good or bad, is just that. Take everything at face value and don't take everything to heart.

This way, compliments will not go to your head and you will not think about the bad things that other people might say.

4. Individualists

For the individualist, you should be able to get a reality check once in a while. Get out of your comfort zone and live in the real world.

Always remember that although you are prone to fantasizing and fear being insignificant, it is important that you live in the real world where you would be able to solve your problems through practical thought and analysis.

This way, you will find important in your life and in other people's. It is also equally significant to have people around you that will bring you back down to earth if ever you find yourself daydreaming again.

Always try to look yourself in reality even when you are dreaming about what you want in life.

You can do this by making attainable goals. For example, if you dream of becoming rich, save up for the future. If you want to have your dream house, invest your earnings wisely.

Your own worst any me is yourself so you just have to be persistent and wise in your decisions. By doing this, you will be able to turn your dreams into reality sooner rather than later.

5. Investigators

For investigators, it is important that you are able to connect with real people as well. Since you have a tendency to be trapped in your mind with the concepts and solutions that you always formulate when trying to solve the mystery, you have to be aware of your surroundings more often.

Always remember that not everyone is out to get you. Be open to the possibility of making new connections so that you may be able to live your life without regret.

6. The Loyalist

Loyalists are prone to worrying a lot. This is ironic because the holy idea that they strive for usually is faith. If you fear to lose the support of other people, then you have to be able to learn how to fend for yourself as this personality type. This way, you can get rid of not wanting to have support all the time. Practice being independent and you will be fine.

7. The Enthusiast

What you need to be careful about as an enthusiast is being stuck planning what you want to do in life and not being able to do anything at all. You have to couple planning with the action.

You also have to try and predict what will happen if you do something. Weigh the pros and cons of your decisions and everything else will turn out for the best.

8. Challenger

This particular personality type has to deal with figuring out history motivations for protecting someone. Are you doing it out of a sense of duty?

Or do you really care about that person? If your motivations are clear then whenever you do in life will be the best decision that you will have made.

Also, be careful that you don't use any of you required skills in life to exact vengeance on other people. If you do this, then your core values will be destroyed.

9. Peacemakers

Peacemakers have a tendency to be locked in a dream state much like the individualist. They always live wanting to do something to change the world, but not actually doing anything to reach their goal.

If you have this personality, you have to make sure that you are able to take action as well as think about how you want to achieve anything in life.

Make sure that everything you do is in service of you reaching that goal. This way, you will be able to realize your dreams more fully down the line.

Chapter 3: The Further Examination of Interpersonal Relationships within the Personality Enneagram

Interpersonal relationships are extremely important during the aforementioned stages of cognitive development for humans because it builds the framework of the entire personality. How people see you will determine how you see yourself and vice versa.

If one does not learn to interact properly during childhood, chances are this may carry over into adulthood and turn the individual into someone who is introverted and quiet. This might be where inferiority complex develops if left unchecked.

It is also during these formative years that a person learns to build significant relationships with people of the same and opposite genders.

How he views himself and others will depend upon the types of connections that he makes all throughout his childhood and during puberty.

More on the Wings of Personality

In addition to this, according to some theorists who support the Enneagram of Personality, the individual-based personality can change depending on the kinds of interactions that he or she experiences.

This change can be brought about more prominently by the interaction of two distinct personalities that are closer to one another in number.

This is what is known as the **Personality Wings.**

For example, the challenge and protector can be tempered by someone who always tries to strive for peace as a mediator. They can learn from one another and make subsequent changes to their personality in terms of how they interact with other people.

These lessons can define the experiences that they would be willing to share together.

The protector can learn that there are other ways of getting things done aside from action and the same thing will happen in reverse for the mediator.

Learning the specific personality type that a person has according to the Enneagram can definitely help improve the quality of interpersonal relationships that a person can have.

Case Study:

Disclaimer: The names and locations in this particular case study have been changed to protect the identity of the concerned individuals.

Marianne grew up with an alcoholic father and an absentee mother due to working overseas. At the age of 19, after having a string of not-so-serious relationships, she eloped with her then boyfriend and got pregnant soon after. They spent a few years together while remaining unattached.

When the child was about five, Marianne decided to return home to her father together with her boyfriend and the child. Though they were provided for, the relationship between Marianne and her boyfriend started to fall apart.

Marianne ended up having to work abroad as well to provide for her family. She replaced her mother as an overseas worker and has been working there for a few years now.

Recently, her teenage daughters decided to leave the apartment they lived in with their grandmother and uncle because of a huge fight they had.

Apparently, the eldest of the girls is obstinate and will not follow the house rules set by the uncle who had been left to care for the two girls after the grandmother decided to work in the city to gain additional income.

What do you think will become of the two girls? How do you think have their own circumstances affected the way they interacted with the authority figures that had been present in their lives during this time?

Is it safe to say that the two girls would end up having the same fate as their mother in terms of relationships especially with the opposite sex?

Overall Analysis

Though it would still be too soon to tell right now, based on the details shared here, it is easy to surmise that the choices made by the two girls have been brought about by the environment that they grew up in.

They have spent most of their childhood on their own, due to the mother needing to work abroad to support the family because of the father's absence.

Therefore, in those years that they had no one to look after them, but the alcoholic grandfather and then the grandmother after the former's death, they grew up without a proper semblance of authority.

These girls learned to think for themselves and challenge anyone with opposing views irrespective of the source.

The same thing will happen to a child who grows up to be an independent-minded individual. She will learn not to accept authority and will want to be on her own at an early age even if she may not be ready to do so yet.

In this scenario, there is little to no way for the present figures of authority to convince the child to go back to their former apartment. Mainly because she has learned that she did not like living with people who will not let her have her way.

If a child does not learn discipline and respect for authority right from the start, he or she will end up challenging every authority figure that comes her way because she will feel that they are out to infringe on her freedom and anything that she wants to do in her life.

In contrast, if the child grows up in a household that puts emphasis on fostering a loving and respectful environment and family dynamic, he will learn that he can express his opinions freely without having to argue with his loved ones all the time.

He will still be able to assert his freedom while maintaining a loving relationship with his or her parents.

This is why it is important for people to develop meaningful relationships all throughout their lives. One should learn to cultivate respectful interactions that are filled with regular open discussion regarding their lives and the decisions that they normally make.

If parents are able to build an open and loving relationship with their children right from the start, it will certainly shape their personality in a much more positive way even if the parents end up separating or going away for a while.

The constant presence of a strong authority figure to look up to for the children will definitely help in the formation of a healthy personality. There should be a balance between letting the children be on their own and disciplining them in case they do something wrong.

This is where proper behavior modification techniques come in. It will be discussed later in the next few chapters.

Questions to Ponder On

Is it too late to change and modify negative aspects of your personality? This question will be answered later on in the book.

Subchapter 1: Behavior Modification and the Role it plays In Developing the Enneagram of Personality

To answer the question from the previous chapter, it is never too late to change the negative aspects of one's personality. However, it can be very challenging especially if the negative behavior brought about by the unsavory aspects of one's personality is deeply rooted in the individual's psyche.

However, if you truly want to alter parts of your personality there are certain procedures that you can undertake as part of behavior modification.

What is Behavior Modification?

Before going any further, let us first find out the meaning of Behavior Modification.

The term Behavior Modification refers to a form of psychological treatment that works under the premise of Operant Conditioning. This particular procedure works in such a way that it replaces undesirable behavior with much healthier patterns through the use of positive and negative reinforcement.

This treatment was formally introduced by an American behaviorist named B.F. Skinner. This is mostly used on children whose parents would want to train to become more obedient and develop a number of positive traits and behavioral patterns.

2 Different Types of Behavioral Reinforcement

There are many different kinds of behavioral modification techniques. Right now, we will focus on the two major types of reinforcement.

• Positive Reinforcement

One of the most popular forms of behavior modification, it works in such a way that the child is offered a reward for any type of positive behavior that he does.

The reward system is commonly placed within a distinct set of parameters and a controlled environment. In addition, this only works if the child agrees with the set parameters, to begin with.

As an example, imagine the child wanting to have his own mobile phone. As a parent, you can give him a mobile phone as a reward for maintaining stellar grades in school.

- **Negative Reinforcement**

In contrast, the next form of behavior modification is negative reinforcement. If the former utilizes a reward system for the child, this particular type of reinforcement deals with the removal of certain comforts that the child has grown attached to.

For instance, if a child does not do his homework right away after school, the parent can choose to take away his television or computer privileges.

In connection with personality development, both positive and negative reinforcement plays a role in this process by a way of training the child to behave a certain way. Positive or negative aspects of the child's personality eventually may surface because of these techniques into adulthood.

For example, a child who grows up to be timid and afraid of confrontation may have experienced corporal punishment as part of his personal set of parental discipline techniques as a child.

There are many other kinds of behavior modification techniques which will be discussed later in the book along with different types of personality disorders and possible treatment methods.

While some experts may view this as an unhealthy way to reinforce certain behaviors, it has been proven effective in reinforcing the desired behavioral patterns in a child.

I think what is most important is that the parent is able to explain why he feels the need to subject the child to different kinds of behavior modification techniques.

By doing this, the child will not end up resenting the parent for taking away or providing what he needs depending on his fulfillment of the conditions set by the parent.

Doing this will also reinforce the positive effect of open communication between the parent and the child. The child will feel comfortable enough to tell the parent about how he feels regarding the reinforcing activities. Changes can effectively be made down the road if and when necessary.

Subchapter 2: The Importance of Meditation

Since discovering your inner personality type has to do with intrinsic conversations and being aware of who you are as a person, it is important that you are able to find inner peace within yourself. One way of doing that is to meditate on a regular basis.

Meditation is one key element in discovering how it is to work with your inner self and thoughts so that you would be able to interact better with other people in the long run.

However, one may ask why is it so important for people to meditate in order to find themselves and discover how to interact better with people? Can't they just do it on their own?

Meditation serves to quiet the mind from the hustle and bustle of the outside world. If you are not able to sit in silence for a few minutes and be one with yourself so to speak, it would be harder for you to understand why other people behave in certain ways which can present challenges for you when it comes to reacting back to certain situations.

This is why it is important for you to think about the situation intently and in silence first before you make a decision as to how to proceed.

Subchapter 3: Meditation in A Few Simple Steps

The first step to take would be the center yourself. You can do this by taking a few deep breaths; inhale and exhale. This will help clear the mind and become more open to the possibility of connecting with other wings of personality that are closer to yours.

You can do this for about 5 minutes. Afterward, you can close your eyes and reflect on what makes your personality different and similar to another personality type in the Enneagram.

For example, if you are a Reformer, this could be the proper time for you to reflect on how you interact with your personality wing.

For Reformers, they are generally closer to those who are helpers. They easily tend to form a bond to these particular types of personality. Through meditation, you will come to understand why this is so and how you can further develop this particular bond to build relationships with others in your circle as well.

Based on the personality types, the most likely individual to undergo meditation on a regular basis would be the Mediator or Peacemaker. This is because of their own goal for existence which is wholeness and peace of mind.

Meditation is known for allowing practitioners to be able to see clearly as to what they are supposed to do in life.

Finding your main purpose as mentioned earlier will help you become a much better individual which can lead to better interactions between you and the other personalities on a regular basis.

Subchapter 4: More Queries and Answers

What makes priests and monks more spiritually able to connect with other people? How do their personalities differ from other individuals?

To answer these questions, we have to understand the motivations of these particular individuals. As mentioned in previous chapters, mediators or peacemakers tend to deal with people's emotions on a much more direct level.

They are sensitive creatures that are able to channel emotions in a much deeper sense.

This strong sensitivity allows people of these personality types to help others in a way that is more profound and effective in the long run. The question is why is this so? Why are the more attuned to people's emotions than other individuals? What makes them so special?

The answer is meditation. People with the ninth personality type are able to understand people better because they have been through the same experiences most of the time.

As they say, people who have been through a lot of hardship and difficulty grow up to be the kindest and compassionate souls there are.

This holds true because most of these individuals know how it feels to be without so that when they encountered similarly situated people, they instantly are able to build a connection and help them whenever necessary.

What about the other personality types? How are they able to find their own purpose and road to personal development? The answer to this question depends on each individual situation that a person with a specific personality type finds himself in.

It really depends on the different choices and people certain individuals interact within their lifetime.

If you truly want to find your purpose, it is important that you are able to experience life without limits. By doing this, you will be able to find out what you can and cannot do and how to deal with various challenges in life.

Through these challenges, you will learn how to modify your behavior according to each and every situation.

In addition to this, if you want to help others change for the better, you can also apply the aforementioned behavior modification techniques to help them discover what needs to be changed and modify their reactions in a positive manner.

Conclusion

The Overall Components of Human Personality and the Importance of Parental Supervision

While it is true that our own choices and environment help shape our own personality construct, our childhood experiences and the people that surrounded us during this time also play a significant role in our development as an individual.

It is during the significant stages of human development that parental oversight and guidance is greatly needed. The parental presence or lack thereof will determine what the child will become in terms of his personality development.

Will he end up succumbing to his sexual desires above all else? Or will he learn to control himself and become a mature and capable human being?

The question of nature vs. nurture definitely is something that can cause debate among various experts. The belief that personality comes from the intrinsic values of the individual as opposed to how he was raised and the quality of the environment that he lived in during infancy in regards to personality formation warrants the need for further research.

One thing is for sure though, the presence of an authority figure helps guide an individual into the road that he is bound to take during adulthood.

Whether it be the parents or an older guardian, adult supervision is quite important when it comes to personality development as a whole.

Throughout the years, there have been many schools of thought purported relating to the components of human personality. This is why it is important to learn the basic components of human personality and how it relates to one another.

The Enneagram helps the common individual understand what makes up a complete personality and how people can relate to one another in terms of interpersonal relationships.

We hope that the various sections of the book helped the reader understand the Enneagram of personality as part of the whole psychological exploration. It is also our hope that the reader learns to interact with society in a much better fashion through the book.

Always remember that by discovering who you are, you will be able to understand the world around you as well as the people who inhabit it. This will make it easier for you to handle various challenges in life as they come.

In addition, challenges and relationships make people better as they age. Instead of shying away from it, you must always be ready to embrace and accept them as part of life. Then and only then can you mature and truly grow as a complete individual.

It is our differences that make this unique and our similarities and that help us connect with one another. One should never change who he is, but always try to discover his real motivations in life.

These motivations will carry him through and help him understand why he reacts a certain way to things that are out of his control.

No matter what personality type you have, this is what you should strive for. To know who you are and to help others discover and unlock their true potential in this journey called life. You will certainly not regret making this your mission in life.

Disclaimer

The information contained in **"Practical Emotional Intelligence & The Enneagram Of Personality -2 In 1-"** and its components, is meant to serve as a comprehensive collection of strategies that the author of this eBook has done research about. Summaries, strategies, tips and tricks are only recommendations by the author, and reading this eBook will not guarantee that one's results will exactly mirror the author's results.

The author of this Ebook has made all reasonable efforts to provide current and accurate information for the readers of this eBook. The author and its associates will not be held liable for any unintentional errors or omissions that may be found.

The material in the Ebook may include information by third parties. Third party materials comprise of opinions expressed by their owners. As such, the author of this eBook does not assume responsibility or liability for any third party material or opinions.

The publication of third party material does not constitute the author's guarantee of any information, products, services, or opinions contained within third party material. Use of third party material does not guarantee that your results will mirror our results. Publication of such third party material is simply a recommendation and expression of the author's own opinion of that material.

Whether because of the progression of the Internet, or the unforeseen changes in company policy and editorial submission guidelines, what is stated as fact at the time of this writing may become outdated or inapplicable later.